*For your entertainment, enjoyment and educational pleasure,
we are presenting:*

The Jewish Trivia
& Information Book™:

Trivia Judaica™

ENDORSED BY BLU GREENBERG
President, JWB Jewish Book Council

► "A delightful book filled with not-so-trivial information."
— *Blu Greenberg*

Featuring:

► Many thousands of new challenging and thought provoking questions.
► On 8 popular Jewish subjects.
► Presenting Factual and Historical Information on Jewish Current Events, Jewish Arts and Culture, Jewish Personalities, Jewish Religion, Jewish History, Jewish Language and Jewish Geography.
► Strengthens and broadens the knowledge of one's Jewish heritage.

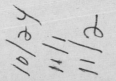

The Most Challenging, Enjoyable and
Educational Judaica Book ever written.

The Jewish Trivia & Information Book™

Trivia Judaica™

BY IAN SHAPOLSKY

Published by Steimatzky Inc., New York.

STEIMATZKY

New York   Jerusalem   Tel Aviv

A Steimatzky Book
Published by Steimatzky N.Y.

Typesetting by First Galley Typography, New York City, NY

1st Edition Sept. 1984
2nd Printing Oct. 1984

ISBN 965-236007-4

DEDICATION

For my parents, Anita and Meyer, whose help was appreciated.

For my sister Lisa, and her family.

—I.S.

New York Jerusalem
Tel Aviv

ACKNOWLEDGEMENTS

This research project was greatly facilitated by the generous assistance of Rabbi Nathan Goldberg, who helped clarify some of the more difficult Talmudic interpretations and language translations that were covered in this book. Rabbi Richard Chapin was also helpful at the inception of the project by pointing me in the right direction for source materials.

I would also like to express my sincere thanks for the countless hours of generous help I received from the various librarians in the Judaica departments of the many New York City libraries visited in this project. They were all tremendously helpful in assisting me to find the correct research materials necessary for this endeavor.

The research editors of this project, led by Bruce Whyte, were indispensable and did a superb job.

The assistant editors, led by Judy Friedman, were equally indispensable in their dedication to the completion of this project.

Lastly, I would like to acknowledge and thank Mordechai Shein for the unlimited amounts of assistance and guidance that he provided. His insights and recommendations were invaluable to me. I also must thank his wife and son for lending him to me for all of those hours that he should have been home with them!

FOREWORD

I hope that you get many pleasurable hours of educational entertainment from reading this book and testing your knowledge of Judaica.

The book is divided into seven easy-to-read categories of questions and answers on each page. Because of this structure, it is especially well suited for use as a quiz book among groups of people who think they are knowledgeable about Jewish subjects. Challenge your friends and family and discover who truly is informed on subjects of Jewish interest!

If any reader has any comments or suggestions on new questions, I would appreciate hearing from you and I will carefully consider your questions for forthcoming editions.

If your question or questions are accepted, you will be credited in the next edition of the book — and you will receive a $5.00 gift certificate towards the purchase of any books available in the Steimatzky Book Agency of North America.

Please address all responses to:
Trivia Judaica Contest
Steimatzky Agency Inc.
P.O. Box 1301, New York, NY 10156
or call the New York office at (212) 505-2505.

 STEIMATZKY

New York   Jerusalem   Tel Aviv

CURRENT
EVENTS

1. ► What happened to the Israeli orange crop in 1978, that made headlines?

ARTS &
CULTURES

2. ► This Jewish author wrote *The Feminine Mystique*, which helped to propel America's feminist movement...?

PEOPLE

3. ► Who ordered the bombing of the *Altalena*, a ship carrying arms to the Irgun, in 1948?

RELIGION

4. ► What was the Biblical structure *Tabernacle* referring to?

HISTORY

5. ► The Wailing Wall was off limits to Jews because this country would not allow them to worship there, in violation of the Armistice Agreement?

LANGUAGE

6. ► What are the two ways that the vowel sounds are written in Hebrew?

GEOGRAPHY

7. ► What country is directly east of Israel?

ANSWERS

CURRENT
EVENTS 1. ▶ Palestinian terrorists placed poison in the oranges, temporarily halting sales.

ARTS &
CULTURES 2. ▶ Betty Friedan.

PEOPLE 3. ▶ David Ben Gurion (in what he claimed was one of the most difficult decisions of his life).

RELIGION 4. ▶ A portable building that held the Ark of the Covenant during the Jews' wanderings in the desert.

HISTORY 5. ▶ Jordan (Jordanian authorities would not allow international access to the Jewish Holy Places under their control).

LANGUAGE 6. ▶ Dots and dashes.

GEOGRAPHY 7. ▶ Jordan.

CURRENT
EVENTS

8. ► In September 1977, he made history by addressing Israel's Knesset...?

ARTS &
CULTURES

9. ► The Jewish founder of Simon & Schuster publishing house, Richard Simon, is the father of this famous singer-songwriter...?

PEOPLE

10. ► She was the only Jewish "Miss America"...?

RELIGION

11. ► The Biblical significance of the location "Ararat" was...?

HISTORY

12. ► Jerusalem was given a special status according to the 1947 U.N. Partition Resolution. What was the major problem with implementing this special status?

LANGUAGE

13. ► What is the language of origin for the names of the Jewish months?

GEOGRAPHY

14. ► What was the name of the mountain upon which Moses viewed the Promised Land?

ANSWERS

CURRENT
EVENTS

8. ► **President Anwar Sadat, of Egypt.**

ARTS &
CULTURES

9. ► **Carly Simon.**

PEOPLE

10. ► **Bess Myerson (in 1945).**

RELIGION

11. ► **The mountain where Noah's Ark landed.**

HISTORY

12. ► **It was not accepted by the Arabs (Jerusalem was made into an international city but this was never enforced).**

LANGUAGE

13. ► **Babylonian.**

GEOGRAPHY

14. ► **Nebo.**

4

CURRENT
EVENTS

15. ▶ In 1977, what Arab nation was the first to participate at the World Jewish Congress in N.Y.?

ARTS &
CULTURES

16. ▶ This Jewish film-maker is the highest dollar-grossing director in history...?

PEOPLE

17. ▶ This man has come to be known as "The Voice of Israel"...?

RELIGION

18. ▶ Who said: "Am I my brother's keeper?", and who did he say it to?

HISTORY

19. ▶ The British were victorious in their battle over Jerusalem, in December of 1917, against which opponent?

LANGUAGE

20. ▶ What is the original meaning of the German word for synagogue, *Schul*?

GEOGRAPHY

21. ▶ The famous Biblical and Talmudic scholar, Rashi, lived in this country...?

ANSWERS

CURRENT
EVENTS   15. ► Morocco.

ARTS &
CULTURES   16. ► Steven Spielberg.

PEOPLE   17. ► Abba Eban.

RELIGION   18. ► Cain said it to G-d when G-d asked where his brother Abel was.

HISTORY   19. ► The Turks.

LANGUAGE   20. ► School. (In earlier times the synagogue was the center of Jewish education as well as religion.)

GEOGRAPHY   21. ► France.

CURRENT
EVENTS

22. ► What publicized event transpired in the Munich Military Academy, in 1977, that surprised Jews throughout the world?

ARTS &
CULTURES

23. ► What is the main curriculum at Dropsie College, located in Philadelphia, PA...?

PEOPLE

24. ► What Jewish lawyer defended the "Chicago Seven"?

RELIGION

25. ► This Biblical quotation: "The Lord is my shepherd, I shall not want" is found in the Book of...?

HISTORY

26. ► The famous French case involving the Jewish Captain Alfred Dreyfus was flawed, and he was eventually found innocent because of this discovery...?

LANGUAGE

27. ► How many vowels are there in the Hebrew language?

GEOGRAPHY

28. ► Where can Israel's wilderness of "Zin" be found?

ANSWERS

22. ► It was revealed that German Officers at the Academy participated in a symbolic burning of Jews by burning pieces of papers.

23. ► A language school for the study of Hebrew and related languages.

24. ► William Kunstler.

25. ► Psalms.

26. ► The letter used to prove his guilt and conspiracy was proved to be a forgery.

27. ► Six.

28. ► In the Negev.

CURRENT EVENTS

29. ► What did an Israeli ship pick up off the Vietnam coast and bring to Israel, in 1977?

ARTS & CULTURES

30. ► This Hebrew king is found in Oscar Wilde's *Salome*...?

PEOPLE

31. ► He was the only non-Israeli Arab to address the Israeli Knesset...?

RELIGION

32. ► What do the *Tefillin* and the *Mezuzah* have in common?

HISTORY

33. ► This Roman Emperor's army was responsible for the destruction of Jerusalem in 135 C.E....?

LANGUAGE

34. ► What does *Baruch Ha'Shem* mean?

GEOGRAPHY

35. ► What was the Biblical "Tower of David" a symbol of?

ANSWERS

CURRENT
EVENTS 29. ► Vietnamese boat people (66 of them).

ARTS &
CULTURES 30. ► Herod.

PEOPLE 31. ► President Anwar Sadat of Egypt, in 1977.

RELIGION 32. ► They both contain parchment with the same verses from the Bible on them.

HISTORY 33. ► Hadrian.

LANGUAGE 34. ► "Blessed be G-d", meaning one is doing well thanks to G-d's good will.

GEOGRAPHY 35. ► Power.

CURRENT
EVENTS

36. ► What did the Hanafi Muslim group do in 1977, in Washington, D.C., that upset the Jewish world?

ARTS &
CULTURES

37. ► In what American movie about the Russian revolution does Polish-Jewish author Jerzy Kosinski briefly appear?

PEOPLE

38. ► This Jewish U.S. economist was invited in 1977, by the Israeli government, to serve as its economic advisor...?

RELIGION

39. ► The Talmud was compiled twice — at two different times and in two different places. Name the two different variations of the Talmud...?

HISTORY

40. ► This famous British General was victorious in his entry into Jerusalem, in December of 1917...?

LANGUAGE

41. ► A *Meshumad* is...?

GEOGRAPHY

42. ► What direction do the Jews of Safed, Israel face when they pray?

ANSWERS

CURRENT EVENTS
36. ► They attacked the headquarters of the B'nai B'rith and took hostages.

ARTS & CULTURES
37. ► *Reds.*

PEOPLE
38. ► Milton Friedman.

RELIGION
39. ► The Babylonian and the Jerusalem Talmud.

HISTORY
40. ► General Allenby.

LANGUAGE
41. ► One who renounces Judaism and takes another religion for material consideration.

GEOGRAPHY
42. ► They face south, which is for them towards Jerusalem.

CURRENT
EVENTS

43. ► What person involved in the Watergate scandal said, "Those Jewboys are everywhere. You can't stop them."?

ARTS &
CULTURES

44. ► What is the most divisive view of the hard-core extremist Reform movement, concerning Israel?

PEOPLE

45. ► This Jewish politician was elected governor of New York State four times and then became a U.S. Senator...?

RELIGION

46. ► The Five Books of Moses are also called...?

HISTORY

47. ► Poland's economic method of persecuting its Jewish population, prior to World War II, was...?

LANGUAGE

48. ► The Yiddish description of food as *milchig* means...?

GEOGRAPHY

49. ► What does Russia's "Pale of Settlement" refer to?

ANSWERS

CURRENT
EVENTS   43. ► Richard Nixon (to John Dean).

ARTS &
CULTURES   44. ► That Judaism is only a religion and
        should not be a nationality.

PEOPLE   45. ► Herbert Lehman.

RELIGION 46. ► The Torah, or the Scroll of Law.

HISTORY   47. ► Boycotts.

LANGUAGE 48. ► It is milky.

GEOGRAPHY 49. ► The area that Jews were permitted to
        live, in Russia (between the Black Sea
        and the Baltic area), up until the Rus-
        sian Revolution.

14

CURRENT
EVENTS
    50. ▶ The year 1984 corresponds to which year or years according to the Jewish calendar?

ARTS &
CULTURES
    51. ▶ This American-Jewish poet wrote a Sonnet, *The Colossus*, found on a famous American landmark...?

PEOPLE
    52. ▶ What Cabinet member, who served in both the Ford and Carter administrations, converted from Judaism to become a Lutheran, when he was younger?

RELIGION
    53. ▶ This prophet was called "The Chariots and the Horsemen of Israel"...?

HISTORY
    54. ▶ Which German monarchy gave the Jewish population equal rights in 1812?

LANGUAGE
    55. ▶ The word *Hebrew*, as used to refer to Abraham in the Bible, means...?

GEOGRAPHY
    56. ▶ This city has the largest Jewish population in South Africa...?

ANSWERS

CURRENT
EVENTS

50. ► Between the years 5744 and 5745.

ARTS &
CULTURES

51. ► Emma Lazarus (her poem is found on the Statue of Liberty).

PEOPLE

52. ► James Schlesinger.

RELIGION

53. ► Elijah.

HISTORY

54. ► Prussia.

LANGUAGE

55. ► "He who crossed over" (referring to Abraham's crossing of the Euphrates River to reach the Promised Land.

GEOGRAPHY

56. ► Johannesburg.

CURRENT
EVENTS

57. ► This man was the second Jew and the first non-American born, ever to hold a U.S. Cabinet post...?

ARTS &
CULTURES

58. ► This fictional hypnotist was presented to the public as a Jew...?

PEOPLE

59. ► This "Symbol of Israel's government" once said: "Give me all the ideologies and values in the world on one hand and the security of Israel on the other, and I'll take the second. Without our physical survival, these ideologies and values have no meaning...the dead do not praise the Lord."...?

RELIGION

60. ► What is the moral of the Biblical story of Abraham's willingness to sacrifice his son, Isaac, because of an order from G-d?

HISTORY

61. ► In what year were the Jews of Spain expelled by King Ferdinand?

LANGUAGE

62. ► What is the derivation of the word "Jew"?

GEOGRAPHY

63. ► What was the first Jewish city in Israel, founded in 1909?

ANSWERS

CURRENT
EVENTS
57. ► Henry Kissinger.

ARTS &
CULTURES
58. ► Svengali.

PEOPLE
59. ► David Ben Gurion.

RELIGION
60. ► He passed G-d's test of faith and the Jewish people were, therefore, rewarded with eternal survival.

HISTORY
61. ► 1492.

LANGUAGE
62. ► From the Biblical location Judah.

GEOGRAPHY
63. ► Tel Aviv (originally named "Ahuzat Bait").

CURRENT
EVENTS

64. ► What significant world event occurred on October 6, 1973?

ARTS &
CULTURES

65. ► Name the Broadway musical that was partially based on the real life romance between the two Jewish songwriters and composers who also scored the play...?

PEOPLE

66. ► In 1916, President Woodrow Wilson appointed this Jewish lawyer to a judicial post and arose the largest wave of opposition in the history of judicial appointments...?

RELIGION

67. ► The symbolic value of the *Succah* hut is...?

HISTORY

68. ► What was the ancient Hebrew measure for the distance from one's forearm to the tip of one's finger, called?

LANGUAGE

69. ► These Hebrew names—*Ir David* and *Ir Hashalom*—refer to the same place, Jerusalem, although they mean different things. What do they mean in English?

GEOGRAPHY

70. ► What "Gate" in Jerusalem is named for an animal?

ANSWERS

64. ▶ Egypt and Syria launched simultaneous attacks on Israel, beginning the Yom Kippur War.

65. ▶ *They're Playing Our Song* (scored by Marvin Hamlisch and Carol Bayer Sager).

66. ▶ Louis Brandeis (appointed to the U.S. Supreme Court).

67. ▶ It is a reminder of the hardship and rough living conditions that the Jews suffered, in their 40 years of wandering in the desert.

68. ▶ The cubit.

69. ▶ *Ir David* means "City of David"; *Ir Hashalom* means "City of Peace."

70. ▶ "Lion's Gate."

CURRENT
EVENTS

71. ► President Kennedy appointed him as Secretary of Labor and then appointed him to the Supreme Court...?

ARTS &
CULTURES

72. ► Which American university had the first Nathan Littauer Chair of Jewish Literature and Philosophy?

PEOPLE

73. ► What famous Israeli Prime Minister was born with the last name "Green"?

RELIGION

74. ► The Bible describes the Promised Land by comparing it to these foods...?

HISTORY

75. ► What caused Moses to finally return to Egypt?

LANGUAGE

76. ► This Hebrew word is frequently used by Christians as well as Moslems, when they pray...?

GEOGRAPHY

77. ► In modern times, for how many years was Jerusalem a divided city?

ANSWERS

71. ► Arthur Goldberg.

72. ► Harvard University.

73. ► David Ben Gurion.

74. ► Milk and honey (Exodus).

75. ► The voice of G-d came to him through the Burning Bush and told him to go to Egypt and lead his people to freedom.

76. ► Amen.

77. ► Nineteen years (from 1948 to 1967).

CURRENT
EVENTS

78. ► This controversial Jewish leader founded a Jewish organization, in the 1960's, advocating violence as a viable means of achieving one's goals...?

ARTS &
CULTURES

79. ► Who was the original Tevye, in the Broadway production of *Fiddler on the Roof*?

PEOPLE

80. ► This Jewish thinker was the father of modern psychology?

RELIGION

81. ► These are the three last words of the Passover Seder...?

HISTORY

82. ► How many tribes were there in the Kingdom of Israel and how many in the Kingdom of Judea?

LANGUAGE

83. ► The *Kol Nidre* prayer is not in Hebrew. It is in this language...?

GEOGRAPHY

84. ► Where was King Solomon's navy located?

ANSWERS

CURRENT EVENTS

78. ► Meir Kahane (and the Jewish Defense League).

ARTS & CULTURES

79. ► Zero Mostel.

PEOPLE

80. ► Sigmund Freud.

RELIGION

81. ► *Leshana Haba'a Be-Yerushalayim* (Next Year in Jerusalem).

HISTORY

82. ► Ten in Israel and two in Judea.

LANGUAGE

83. ► Aramaic.

GEOGRAPHY

84. ► On the shores of the Red Sea, in Ezion Geber (Kings).

CURRENT
EVENTS

85. ▶ What action did Anwar Sadat take, in July of 1972, that stunned Egyptian allies even more than the Western world?

ARTS &
CULTURES

86. ▶ This Jewish philosopher wrote in Greek about Judaism and its relation to the prevailing Greek philosophy of his day...?

PEOPLE

87. ▶ This Jewish politician was known as "The busiest man in the U.S. Senate"...?

RELIGION

88. ▶ Abraham and Moses are so special to the Jewish people that they have been given these honored titles, in English, to remind us of their importance...?

HISTORY

89. ▶ The Jewish Resistance Movement was formed in 1945, encompassing these three major Jewish resistance organizations in Palestine...?

LANGUAGE

90. ▶ The adjective *Shaddai* translates into...?

GEOGRAPHY

91. ▶ This place was the first taste of America for many European Jews...?

ANSWERS

CURRENT EVENTS 85. ► He expelled all Russian technical and military advisors from Egypt.

ARTS & CULTURES 86. ► Philo.

PEOPLE 87. ► Jacob Javits.

RELIGION 88. ► Abraham is known as "Our Father," and Moses is known as "Our Teacher."

HISTORY 89. ► The *Hagannah*, the *Etzel (Irgun)* and the *Lechi*.

LANGUAGE 90. ► Almighty.

GEOGRAPHY 91. ► The Ellis Island immigration station.

CURRENT
EVENTS

92. ► The Defense Minister of Israel during the Six-Day War was...?

ARTS &
CULTURES

93. ► Most Yiddish-American writers have followed the model of this famous Russian writer...?

PEOPLE

94. ► Who is the famous Jewish doctor and businessman who originated large-scale trade between the U.S. and Russia?

RELIGION

95. ► The Bible mentions the number 40 in several instances throughout history. Two Biblical situations where the number is relevant are...?

HISTORY

96. ► In this century the Jews were expelled from England...?

LANGUAGE

97. ► What is the meaning of the expression *Moshe Rabbenu*?

GEOGRAPHY

98. ► After the Yom Kippur War, the land captured near the Suez Canal was renamed by Israel, using its original ancient Biblical name...?

ANSWERS

92. ► Moshe Dayan.

ARTS & CULTURES 93. ► Anton Chekov.

PEOPLE 94. ► Dr. Armand Hammer.

RELIGION 95. ► (Any two of these): The story of the flood with 40 days of rain (Genesis); the reign of King David was for 40 years (Samuel); Moses was on Mount Sinai for 40 days (Exodus); and the Jews wandered in the desert for 40 years (Numbers).

HISTORY 96. ► Thirteenth century (1290).

LANGUAGE 97. ► Moses our Teacher.

GEOGRAPHY 98. ► Goshen.

CURRENT
EVENTS

99. ► On June 7, 1981, Israeli planes attacked, and destroyed this objective deep within hostile Arab territory?

ARTS &
CULTURES

100. ► Ingrid Bergman starred in a recent T.V. movie documentary about this famous Israeli...?

PEOPLE

101. ► The *Ba'al Shem Tov* was famous for founding this movement in 18th century Poland...?

RELIGION

102. ► These Biblical figures were all involved in the same type of work: Gideon, Jephtah, Ehud and Debora...?

HISTORY

103. ► What was the British position, if any, on the establishment of a Jewish State after the U.N. Partition Plan was announced in 1947?

LANGUAGE

104. ► What does the Yiddish expression *Feer Kashes* refer to in the Passover Seder?

GEOGRAPHY

105. ► This city could not be conquered by Joshua, but it eventually was conquered by David...?

ANSWERS

CURRENT
EVENTS

99. ► An Iraqi nuclear reactor.

ARTS &
CULTURES

100. ► Golda Meir.

PEOPLE

101. ► Hassidim.

RELIGION

102. ► They were judges.

HISTORY

103. ► They opposed it (refusing to enforce the plan).

LANGUAGE

104. ► The Four Questions.

GEOGRAPHY

105. ► The city of the Jebusites, later known as Jerusalem.

CURRENT
EVENTS

106. ► What was the main reason that the 1983 Israel-Lebanon troop withdrawal plan fell through?

ARTS &
CULTURES

107. ► What 80+-year-old Jewish comedian-actor was born with the name Nathan Birnbaum?

PEOPLE

108. ► In 1930's Palestine he was known as *Ha-Yedid* ("The Friend")...?

RELIGION

109. ► Most of the Biblical judges were chosen from this Tribe of Israel...?

HISTORY

110. ► This Russian monarch formed the "Society of Israelitish Christians," to convert the Jews of Russia...?

LANGUAGE

111. ► The Hebrew translation of the Western Wall is...?

GEOGRAPHY

112. ► The "Damascus Gate" of Jerusalem's Old City leads to which quarter of the city?

ANSWERS

CURRENT
EVENTS

106. ► Syrian President Hafez el Assad refused to agree to a simultaneous withdrawal of Syrian troops, contrary to the impression he conveyed to the U.S.

ARTS &
CULTURES

107. ► George Burns.

PEOPLE

108. ► Captain Orde Wingate, the British officer who organized and trained the *Haganah* into a disciplined self-defense force.

RELIGION

109. ► Levi.

HISTORY

110. ► Alexander I.

LANGUAGE

111. ► *HaKotel Ha-Ma'aravi.*

GEOGRAPHY

112. ► The Moslem quarter.

CURRENT
EVENTS

113. ► Who was President Johnson referring to in his statement: "If a Jew can serve as spokesman for this country to the world, then one of the goals of the United States has been reached"?

ARTS &
CULTURES

114. ► Michelangelo created a statue of this Jewish Biblical hero that is displayed in Florence, Italy...?

PEOPLE

115. ► This Jewish-American statesman was referred to as "The Brains of the Confederacy"...?

RELIGION

116. ► This prophet is best known for his Messianic predictions...?

HISTORY

117. ► Which ancient judge was a cruel and harsh ruler of the Jews for three years, until he was finally assassinated?

LANGUAGE

118. ► What type of woman is an *Eshet Chayil*?

GEOGRAPHY

119. ► What was planned for Grand Island in upstate New York, in the early 20th century?

ANSWERS

CURRENT EVENTS **113.** ► **Arthur Goldberg.**

ARTS & CULTURES **114.** ► **David.**

PEOPLE **115.** ► **Judah Benjamin.**

RELIGION **116.** ► **Isaiah.**

HISTORY **117.** ► **Abimelech.**

LANGUAGE **118.** ► **A woman of valor.**

GEOGRAPHY **119.** ► **This was considered as a potential homeland for the Jews (it would have been called Ararat).**

CURRENT
EVENTS

120. ► The number of Jews living in Los Angeles is approximately...?

ARTS &
CULTURES

121. ► This famous Jewish author popularized the phrase: "Love means never having to say you're sorry"...?

PEOPLE

122. ► He founded the Americanized Reconstructionist version of Judaism...?

RELIGION

123. ► One who voluntarily abandons Judaism for another religion is called...?

HISTORY

124. ► Whom did Samuel select as the first king of Israel?

LANGUAGE

125. ► The Yiddish term *punim* refers to this part of the body...?

GEOGRAPHY

126. ► There is a famous memorial built on Har Hazikaron, Israel. It is called...?

ANSWERS

120. ▶ 500,000.

121. ▶ Eric Segal (in his novel *Love Story*).

122. ▶ Rabbi Mordechai Kaplan.

123. ▶ An apostate.

124. ▶ Saul.

125. ▶ The face.

126. ▶ *Yad Va'shem*.

CURRENT
EVENTS

127. ► What was the plan that the Arab League member-states issued at the end of their summit conference in Morocco, in September 1982?

ARTS &
CULTURES

128. ► This Jewish artist's work prominently decorates the Hadassah Medical Center in Jerusalem...?

PEOPLE

129. ► He wrote the Israeli national anthem, "Hatikva"...?

RELIGION

130. ► The Orthodox Code of Jewish Law is called...?

HISTORY

131. ► To which country do "Cochin Jews" trace their roots?

LANGUAGE

132. ► The *Luach* is...?

GEOGRAPHY

133. ► After King Solomon died and his kingdom was divided in two, what were the new kingdoms called?

ANSWERS

127. ▶ The "Fez Plan," calling for the creation of an independent Palestinian state on the West Bank, with Jerusalem as its capital, and a "guaranteed peace" in the region.

ARTS & CULTURES 128. ▶ Marc Chagall.

PEOPLE 129. ▶ Naftali Hertz Imber.

RELIGION 130. ▶ *The Shulchan Aruch*.

HISTORY 131. ▶ India.

LANGUAGE 132. ▶ The Hebrew calendar.

GEOGRAPHY 133. ▶ The Kingdom of Judea and the Kingom of Israel.

CURRENT
EVENTS

134. ► When did Menachem Begin first win the office of Prime Minister?

ARTS &
CULTURES

135. ► The initial Defense Minister of Israel during the Lebanon War was...?

PEOPLE

136. ► This Jewish physicist discovered radio waves, and their unit of measurement is named after him...?

RELIGION

137. ► What are the four Expressions of Redemption found in the Bible, referring to the Exodus, which are commemorated by drinking four times?

HISTORY

138. ► At what point did the greatest influx of Jews into Turkey take place?

LANGUAGE

139. ► He began the rebirth of the use of Hebrew letters...?

GEOGRAPHY

140. ► Where was the Reform Judaism movement started?

ANSWERS

CURRENT
EVENTS   **134.** ► **1977.**

ARTS &
CULTURES **135.** ► **Ariel Sharon.**

PEOPLE   **136.** ► **Heinrich Hertz.**

RELIGION **137.** ► **I have: brought out; taken out; re-
          deemed; and delivered.**

HISTORY   **138.** ► **After the expulsion of Jews from
          Spain, in 1492.**

LANGUAGE **139.** ► **Moses Chayim Luzzato.**

GEOGRAPHY **140.** ► **Germany.**

CURRENT
EVENTS

141. ▶ For which seven year period did Golda Meir serve as prime minister?

ARTS &
CULTURES

142. ▶ This Jewish sociologist wrote *Beyond the Melting Pot* with Daniel Patrick Moynihan...?

PEOPLE

143. ▶ What is the German Jewish philosopher Martin Buber remembered for?

RELIGION

144. ▶ What famous Biblical event occurred in Ashkelon?

HISTORY

145. ▶ What were the ancient Hebrews allowed to do in marriage that Jews of modern times are forbidden from doing?

LANGUAGE

146. ▶ What is a synagogue's *purochet*?

GEOGRAPHY

147. ▶ There is a street in Jerusalem named Abarvanel Street, after a 14th century leader of the Jewish people. In what country was he a leader?

ANSWERS

CURRENT
EVENTS **141.** ▶ **1968-1974.**

ARTS &
CULTURES **142.** ▶ **Nathan Glazer.**

PEOPLE **143.** ▶ **He was a mystic.**

RELIGION **144.** ▶ **Samson was captured by the Philistines (in Delila's home town).**

HISTORY **145.** ▶ **They were permitted more than one wife.**

LANGUAGE **146.** ▶ **The curtain covering the Holy Ark (often decorated with an image of the Ten Commandments).**

GEOGRAPHY **147.** ▶ **Spain. (He led the Jews of Spain at the time they were expelled.)**

CURRENT
EVENTS
148. ► What was the reason given for the recall of the Egyptian ambassador to Israel, in 1983?

ARTS &
CULTURES
149. ► This famous fictional Jewish character said: "I am a Jew. Hath not a Jew eyes? Hath not a Jew hands, organs, dimensions, sense, affections, passions..."?

PEOPLE
150. ► What was the name of the Jewish interpreter on Columbus' voyage of discovery, who was also the first man to set foot in the new world?

RELIGION
151. ► Why is *Shavuoth* occassionally referred to as "Pentecost"?

HISTORY
152. ► What was the *Machal*, formed in 1948?

LANGUAGE
153. ► This Hebrew word refers to the expulsion and exile of Jews after the destruction of Jerusalem...?

GEOGRAPHY
154. ► What is the approximate current population of Jerusalem?

ANSWERS

148. ► The massacre of Palestinian civilians in the refugee camps of Sabra and Shatila.

ARTS &
CULTURES 149. ► Shylock, from Shakespeare's *The Merchant of Venice*.

PEOPLE 150. ► Rodrigo Sanches.

RELIGION 151. ► Because it occurs 50 days after the first day of Passover.

HISTORY 152. ► It was an organization of volunteers from the Diaspora, that came to aid Israel during the War of Independence.

LANGUAGE 153. ► *Galuth*.

GEOGRAPHY 154. ► 350,000.

CURRENT
EVENTS

155. ► What did President Reagan propose in his September 1982 "Mideast Initiative" that shocked the Jewish communities of the world?

ARTS &
CULTURES

156. ► How do Sephardic and Ashkenazi Jews differ in their views on naming newborn babies?

PEOPLE

157. ► This Jewish developer was a pioneer of tract housing and has towns in New York and in Pennsylvania named after him...?

RELIGION

158. ► What religious group, other than Judaism, keeps its headquarters in Israel?

HISTORY

159. ► What Prophet predicted that, because of its sins and its attack on the Kingdom of Judea, the Kingdom of Israel would fall?

LANGUAGE

160. ► The respectful expression *Alav Hashalom* means...?

GEOGRAPHY

161. ► The Biblical city of Bethlehem literally translates into?

ANSWERS

155. ► He called for the creation of a Palestinian "entity" on the West Bank and the Gaza Strip, in association with Jordan, and he demanded a freeze on all Jewish settlement activities on the West Bank.

156. ► Sephardic Jews name babies after the living; Ashkenazi Jews name them after the deceased.

157. ► Levitt.

158. ► The Bahai (whose main temple is located in Haifa).

159. ► Isaiah. (He was correct. The Assyrians fought Israel for three years until Israel fell, and the Ten Tribes were dispersed and supposedly disappeared.)

160. ► May he or she rest in peace.

161. ► The "House of Bread."

CURRENT
EVENTS

162. ► This Vienna-born financier gained the public eye as Chairman of the Municipal Assistance Corporation, the agency that saved New York City from bankruptcy, in the mid 1970's...?

ARTS &
CULTURES

163. ► These musical Jewish brothers were the most successful American musical comedy producers of their time...?

PEOPLE

164. ► This Jewish philosopher was called "The G-d-intoxicated Man".

RELIGION

165. ► What did Pharaoh do to punish the Israelites after Moses' request for their freedom?

HISTORY

166. ► In the feudal Christian society of the Middle Ages, what activity of Jewish businessmen made them indispensable to their persecutors?

LANGUAGE

167. ► The mixture of Hebrew and Spanish that is spoken by Spanish and Portuguese Jews is called...?

GEOGRAPHY

168. ► In English the Gulf of Aqaba is also known as...?

ANSWERS

162. ► Felix Rohatyn.

163. ► The Shuberts.

164. ► Baruch Spinoza.

165. ► He made their jobs harder by making them find their own straw to make bricks.

166. ► Money-lending. (Christians at this time were generally forbidden by the Church from lending money for interest.)

167. ► Ladino.

168. ► The Gulf of Eilat.

CURRENT
EVENTS

169. ► Who was Foreign Minister for the second government of Menachem Begin?

ARTS &
CULTURES

170. ► This Jewish composer and trumpeteer is well known for his 1960's Mexican-style band..."

PEOPLE

171. ► He was known as the father of "Political Anti-Semitism...?

RELIGION

172. ► He was the first person born on earth...?

HISTORY

173. ► This Biblical character was known for his courage...?

LANGUAGE

174. ► The color black in Yiddish is...?

GEOGRAPHY

175. ► What Gate in Jerusalem is named after another Middle Eastern capital?

ANSWERS

CURRENT EVENTS	169. ►	Yitzhak Shamir.
ARTS & CULTURES	170. ►	Herb Alpert.
PEOPLE	171. ►	Bismarck.
RELIGION	172. ►	Cain.
HISTORY	173. ►	David.
LANGUAGE	174. ►	*Shvartz.*
GEOGRAPHY	175. ►	Damascus Gate.

CURRENT EVENTS

176. ► What two Israeli government positions did Menachem Begin hold in 1980?

ARTS & CULTURES

177. ► Shylock's daughter was named...?

PEOPLE

178. ► Which Jewish doctor and social scientist wrote *The Interpretation of Dreams*?

RELIGION

179. ► The ancient Hebrew scholars and Torah interpreters, Hillel and Shamai, had mostly opposite interpretations. Using one word to describe each of them, how were they different?

HISTORY

180. ► Throughout history, which, if any, non-Jewish country had Jerusalem as its capital?

LANGUAGE

181. ► What did the ancient Hebrews use to indicate numbers when they wrote?

GEOGRAPHY

182. ► Which American state is about the same size as the State of Israel, prior to the 1967 Six-Day War?

ANSWERS

CURRENT
EVENTS **176.** ▶ **Prime Minister and Defense Minister.**

ARTS &
CULTURES **177.** ▶ **Jessica.**

PEOPLE **178.** ▶ **Sigmund Freud.**

RELIGION **179.** ▶ **Hillel's interpretations were "lenient," Shamai's were "strict".**

HISTORY **180.** ▶ **None.**

LANGUAGE **181.** ▶ **The Hebrew alphabet, each letter having a numeric value.**

GEOGRAPHY **182.** ▶ **New Jersey.**

CURRENT
EVENTS

183. ► What was Israel's Moshe Arens' position before he was appointed Defense Minister?

ARTS &
CULTURES

184. ► This Jewish scholar won the Nobel Prize in Economics in 1970, but is best known for his super-selling *Introduction to Economics* textbook...?

PEOPLE

185. ► What did the Jewish scientist Judah Cresques, otherwise known as the "Map Jew" of medieval Spain, hypothesize before all others?

RELIGION

186. ► What were the original Ten Commandments written on?

HISTORY

187. ► The Hasmonean Dynasty was ruled by the descendants of this Biblical group...?

LANGUAGE

188. ► What group of languages does Hebrew belong to?

GEOGRAPHY

189. ► The highest mountain in Israel is...

ANSWERS

CURRENT EVENTS   183. ► Ambassador to the United States.

ARTS & CULTURES   184. ► Paul Samuelson.

PEOPLE   185. ► That the earth was round (200 years before Copernicus).

RELIGION   186. ► Two stone tablets.

HISTORY   187. ► Maccabees.

LANGUAGE   188. ► The Semitic languages.

GEOGRAPHY   189. ► Mount Hebron.

54

CURRENT
EVENTS

190. ► This Jewish politician from Connecticut was one of the most respected men in the Senate...?

ARTS &
CULTURES

191. ► Jacob Cohen is the original name of this always depressed and harassed comedian...?

PEOPLE

192. ► This Jewish American monetarist economist won the 1976 Nobel Prize in Economics...?

RELIGION

193. ► Which of the three major movements of modern Judaism was the last to have evolved?

HISTORY

194. ► Where and against whom did the "Jewish Legion" fight in World War I?

LANGUAGE

195. ► The Hebrew term *seychel*, used also in Yiddish, refers to this quality...?

GEOGRAPHY

196. ► Before World War II, what city had the largest Jewish population in the world?

ANSWERS

190. ► **Abraham Ribicoff.**

191. ► **Rodney Dangerfield.**

192. ► **Milton Friedman.**

193. ► **The Conservative Movement. The Reform and Orthodox movements were considered extreme, so a "middle ground" approach was created under the leadership of Zechariah Frankel.**

194. ► **They fought in Palestine with General Edmund Allenby against the Turks. (They were American and European volunteers who developed a brilliant fighting record.)**

195. ► **Common sense.**

196. ► **Warsaw, Poland.**

CURRENT
EVENTS

197. ► What personal experience was the famous Jewish civil liberties attorney, Aryeh Neier, writing about in his book *Defending My Enemy?*

ARTS &
CULTURES

198. ► This well-respected Jewish magazine is known as being oriented mainly toward Jewish intellectuals...?

PEOPLE

199. ► This auto tycoon was a famous 20th century anti-Semite...?

RELIGION

200. ► What is the word "Numbers" in the title of the "Book of Numbers" a reference to?

HISTORY

201. ► This famous Jewish scholar and Talmudic interpreter taught the following concepts: "An empty-headed man cannot be fearful of sin. An ignorant person cannot be pious. A bashful man cannot learn, and an impatient man cannot teach."...?

LANGUAGE

202. ► The Yiddish term *Shviger,* refers to this type of a relative...?

GEOGRAPHY

203. ► The Gulf of Eilat is Israel's outlet to what seas?

ANSWERS

CURRENT
EVENTS
197. ▶ Defending the right of the American Nazi Party to march in Skokie, Illinois, in 1978.

ARTS &
CULTURES
198. ▶ *Commentary.*

PEOPLE
199. ▶ Henry Ford.

RELIGION
200. ▶ The census of the population.

HISTORY
201. ▶ Hillel.

LANGUAGE
202. ▶ Father-in-law.

GEOGRAPHY
203. ▶ The Red Sea and the Indian Ocean.

CURRENT
EVENTS

204. ► After the Arabs' military defeat in the 1973 Yom Kippur War, they started a new type of war against Israel. What was it?

ARTS &
CULTURES

205. ► Joe Webster and Lew Fields were famous Jewish entertainers in this medium...?

PEOPLE

206. ► This famous early American statesman wrote an important letter to the Jewish population of the original United States promising: "May the children of the stock of Abraham who dwell in this land enjoy the goodwill of the other inhabitants, while everyone shall sit in safety...and there shall be none to make him afraid"...?

RELIGION

207. ► What does the designation "pareve" refer to?

HISTORY

208. ► During what years in modern times was Jerusalem a divided city?

LANGUAGE

209. ► What does *Haggadah* mean?

GEOGRAPHY

210. ► After the death of King Solomon, Jerusalem was the capital of this kingdom...?

ANSWERS

CURRENT
EVENTS

204. ► **Economic war. They applied an oil boycott to any country supporting Israel.**

ARTS &
CULTURES

205. ► **Vaudeville.**

PEOPLE

206. ► **George Washington (in the late 1700's).**

RELIGION

207. ► **Kosher foods that are neither meat nor dairy.**

HISTORY

208. ► **1948 to 1967.**

LANGUAGE

209. ► **Story.**

GEOGRAPHY

210. ► **Judah.**

CURRENT
EVENTS
     211. ► This Jewish politician became mayor of San Francisco, in 1978...?

ARTS &
CULTURES
     212. ► Jewish immigrants from this country brought the Yiddish theater to America...?

PEOPLE
     213. ► Victor Kugler hid a Jewish family from the Nazis for 25 months. Who were they?

RELIGION
     214. ► What was the tenth plague Moses visited upon the Egyptians?

HISTORY
     215. ► This English leader allowed the Jews to return to England...?

LANGUAGE
     216. ► The proper response to the Hebrew greeting *Sholom Aleichem* is...?

GEOGRAPHY
     217. ► What American city is most analogous to Jerusalem?

ANSWERS

CURRENT
EVENTS
    211. ► Dianne Feinstein.

ARTS &
CULTURES
    212. ► Russia.

PEOPLE
    213. ► The family of Anne Frank.

RELIGION
    214. ► The death of all first-born Egyptian males.

HISTORY
    215. ► Oliver Cromwell.

LANGUAGE
    216. ► *Aleichem Sholom.*

GEOGRAPHY
    217. ► Washington, D.C. (It is a capital city, with famous historic landmarks, and museums.)

CURRENT
EVENTS

218. ► What segment or group is Jewish analyst David Garth a guru of?

ARTS &
CULTURES

219. ► He was the evil Jewish character in Dickens' *Oliver Twist*...?

PEOPLE

220. ► He founded the Reform Jewish movement in America...?

RELIGION

221. ► Name the 12 Minor Prophets...?

HISTORY

222. ► Of what origin or classification were the first Jews who came to America?

LANGUAGE

223. ► The Yiddish words *Bobbeh* and *Zaydeh* mean...?

GEOGRAPHY

224. ► Where can these words be found and which Jewish poet wrote them: "Keep ancient lands, your storied pomp. Cries she with silent lips. Give me your tired, your poor, your huddled masses yearning to breathe free, The wretched refuse of your teeming shore, Send these, the homeless, tempest-tossed, to me, I lift my lamp beside the golden door!"?

ANSWERS

CURRENT EVENTS	218. ▶	Politicians.
ARTS & CULTURES	219. ▶	Fagan.
PEOPLE	220. ▶	Isaac Mayer Wise.
RELIGION	221. ▶	Hosea, Amos, Obadiah, Joel, Micah, Jonah, Malachi, Haggai, Zachariah, Zephaniah, Nahum, Habbakuk.
HISTORY	222. ▶	Sephardic.
LANGUAGE	223. ▶	Grandmother and Grandfather.
GEOGRAPHY	224. ▶	The base of the Statue of Liberty, written by Emma Lazarus.

CURRENT
EVENTS
225. ► Elected in 1982, this Jewish U.S. Senator from New Jersey was a past chairman of the United Jewish Appeal and also founded the ADP Corporation...?

ARTS &
CULTURES
226. ► What event inspired Shakespeare to write *The Merchant of Venice?*

PEOPLE
227. ► This Jewish financier was a major supporter of the American Revolution...?

RELIGION
228. ► Of the two original forms of the Talmud, this one is considered the more authoritative...?

HISTORY
229. ► Under which Russian czar were the worst pograms committed?

LANGUAGE
230. ► The term *Rebbetzin* refers to...?

GEOGRAPHY
231. ► In the Six-Day War, Israeli soldiers entered the Old City of Jerusalem through this Gate...?

ANSWERS

CURRENT EVENTS 225. ► Frank B. Lautenberg.

ARTS & CULTURES 226. ► The execution of a Portuguese Jew, Rodrigo Lopez, who was accused of treason.

PEOPLE 227. ► Hayim Salomon.

RELIGION 228. ► The Babylonian.

HISTORY 229. ► Alexander III.

LANGUAGE 230. ► A Rabbi's wife.

GEOGRAPHY 231. ► Lion's Gate.

CURRENT
EVENTS

232. ► Who was the original Israeli defense minister during the invasion of Lebanon?

ARTS &
CULTURES

233. ► This Jewish pop-star explored Jewish themes in his movie *The Jazz Singer*. . .?

PEOPLE

234. ► Dizengoff Road in Tel Aviv is named after Meir Dizengoff. Who was he in Israeli politics?

RELIGION

235. ► How many Psalms are there?

HISTORY

236. ► This Biblical character was known for his wisdom. . .?

LANGUAGE

237. ► A *shtarker* in Yiddish is one who is. . .?

GEOGRAPHY

238. ► In which part of Jerusalem is the Old City located?

ANSWERS

CURRENT EVENTS   **232.** ▶ **Ariel Sharon.**

ARTS & CULTURES   **233.** ▶ **Neil Diamond.**

PEOPLE   **234.** ▶ **The first mayor of Tel Aviv.**

RELIGION   **235.** ▶ **One hundred and fifty.**

HISTORY   **236.** ▶ **Solomon.**

LANGUAGE   **237.** ▶ **Brave or strong.**

GEOGRAPHY   **238.** ▶ **East Jerusalem.**

CURRENT
EVENTS

239. ▶ Which non-Jewish Israeli residents serve in the Israeli Defense Forces?

ARTS &
CULTURES

240. ▶ What edible substance is commonly referred to as "Jewish penicillin"?

PEOPLE

241. ▶ This ancient king said: "A good person is like a tree planted by the streams of water"...?

RELIGION

242. ▶ During what holiday are *challah* and apples dipped in honey and eaten, and why?

HISTORY

243. ▶ In which century did Jews first settle in Pennsylvania?

LANGUAGE

244. ▶ The Hebrew name "Israel" originally translated into...?

GEOGRAPHY

245. ▶ Name two major uses derived from Israel's Negev Desert...?

ANSWERS

239. ► The Druse. (They insisted on being drafted and consider themselves distinct from the Arab population of the Mideast region.)

ARTS & CULTURES

240. ► Chicken soup.

PEOPLE

241. ► King David.

RELIGION

242. ► During Rosh Hashanah, to symbolically allow for a sweet year.

HISTORY

243. ► The seventeenth.

LANGUAGE

244. ► He who battled with an angel, and won. (The name was originally given to Patriarch Jacob by G-d.)

GEOGRAPHY

245. ► (Any two of these): Four annual vegetable harvests; tremendous mineral wealth; tremendous solar energy potential; and it serves as a gateway to the southern Port city of Eilat.

CURRENT
EVENTS
    246. ► Name one of the three additional holidays that have been added to the Jewish calendar in recent times...?

ARTS &
CULTURES
    247. ► This Jewish composer was referred to as the "Dean of American Composers" and he incorporated American tunes and Jewish musical themes into his works...?

PEOPLE
    248. ► He was the anti-Semitic leader of the Spanish Inquisition and was the central figure in the persecution and expulsion of Jews from Spain...?

RELIGION
    249. ► What are the three major ancient divisions of the Jewish tribes?

HISTORY
    250. ► Which Jewish resistance group was responsible for the destruction of the King David Hotel in Jerusalem?

LANGUAGE
    251. ► What is the Yiddish word *gragger*?

GEOGRAPHY
    252. ► What and where is "Birobidjan"?

ANSWERS

CURRENT
EVENTS 246. ► (Any one of these): Yom Yeru-
shalayim (Jerusalem Day); Yom
Hazikaron (Memorial Day for the
Holocaust); Yom Ha-atzmaut (Day of
Israeli Independence).

ARTS &
CULTURES 247. ► Aaron Copland.

PEOPLE 248. ► Torquemada.

RELIGION 249. ► The Levites, the Kohanites, and the
Israelites.

HISTORY 250. ► The Irgun (Etzel).

LANGUAGE 251. ► A noise-making rattle, used on Purim
to create noise at the mention of
Haman's name.

GEOGRAPHY 252. ► An area in the Eastern U.S.S.R., on the
border of China, that was at one time
designated by the Soviets for "au-
tonomous" Jewish settlement.

CURRENT
EVENTS

253. ► Where does the P.L.O. get most of its recruits?

ARTS &
CULTURES

254. ► In Michelangelo's famous sculpture, what non-human characteristic does Moses possess?

PEOPLE

255. ► It is well known that Edison invented the gramophone, which used cylinders, but what Jewish scientist invented the phonograph which used disks?

RELIGION

256. ► What book from the Apocrypha relates the story of *Chanukah*?

HISTORY

257. ► What was the last empire to control Palestine, before the creation of the modern State of Israel?

LANGUAGE

258. ► What is the Biblical injuction called *Zhatnez*?

GEOGRAPHY

259. ► The Port of Jerusalem is called...?

ANSWERS

253. ► Palestinian refugee camps.

254. ► A horned forehead. (Michelangelo misunderstood the use of the word "keren" which means both "to shine" and "horn," in his instructions. Moses' forehead was intended to shine, not to be horned.)

255. ► Emil Berliner.

256. ► The Book of the Maccabees.

257. ► The British Empire.

258. ► A prohibition against mixing wool and linen together in clothing manufacture.

259. ► Jaffa.

CURRENT
EVENTS

260. ► What makes Israel politically unique in the Middle East?

ARTS &
CULTURES

261. ► This Jewish writer is one of the most widely read and the funniest of the social and political satirists today. He highlights the ridiculousness of the American way of life...?

PEOPLE

262. ► This Pope issued a decree ordering the Jews to wear "Badges of Shame"...?

RELIGION

263. ► Name three of the seven Universal Laws of Noah,' or "The Noachite Laws"...?

HISTORY

264. ► What was the purpose of the "Cities of Refuge," established in early Biblical days?

LANGUAGE

265 ► The popular Yiddish word for a spinning top is...?

GEOGRAPHY

266. ► Where, and in what year, did this famous Jewish revolt against the Nazis take place...?

ANSWERS

260. ▶ It is the only democracy.

261. ▶ Art Buchwald.

262. ▶ Pope Innocent III.

263. ▶ (Any three of these): The Laws forbid: idol worship, adultery, bloodshed, stealing, profaning G-d, cutting off a live animal's limb; and the laws between "man and man".

264. ▶ To protect those who accidentally committed murder from vengeance.

265. ▶ *Dreidel.*

266. ▶ The Warsaw Ghetto Uprising, occurred in 1943.

CURRENT
EVENTS

267. ► What country, beginning in 1976, suffered a bloody civil war resulting in over 60,000 casualties, due to the presence of the P.L.O.?

ARTS &
CULTURES

268. ► In which area of science have the Jews made the most contribution?

PEOPLE

269. ► What Israeli leader was born in the Crimea yet fought as an officer in the Turkish Army?

RELIGION

270. ► The name of the Jewish mystical movement is...?

HISTORY

271. ► What is the ancient Story of the Elephants, and who used them against the rebellious Jews?

LANGUAGE

272. ► What country does the Yiddish term *Goldene Medinah* refer to?

GEOGRAPHY

273. ► When the Jews were expelled from Spain, what country, that had just forcibly gained its independence from Spain, welcomed them?

ANSWERS

CURRENT EVENTS **267.** ► Lebanon.

ARTS & CULTURES **268.** ► Medicine.

PEOPLE **269.** ► Moshe Sharett.

RELIGION **270.** ► The "Kabbalah".

HISTORY **271.** ► The King of Syria, Antiochus, thought that the revolt of the Maccabees would be ended when they saw frightening elephants, never before viewed in the Land of Israel. Instead, the Maccabees shot them with arrows, causing them to fall upon the Syrian soldiers.

LANGUAGE **272.** ► The U.S. or "The Golden Land," reflecting the high hopes that immigrants had for America.

GEOGRAPHY **273.** ► Holland.

274. ► The Arabs held a summit conference in Khartoum in 1969, and issued a joint declaration. What was this famous six-word, three-part declaration?

275. ► This author's stories inspired the Broadway musical *Fiddler on the Roof*...?

276. ► Sherry Lansing, of Jewish birth, was the first American woman to ever achieve this position...?

277. ► Identify the two significant floating arks mentioned in the Bible...?

278. ► In 1941, the "Palmach" organization was formed in Palestine, in anticipation of this contingency...?

279. ► The Yiddish word for "pray" is...?

280. ► This country is known as the Jewish capital of South America...?

ANSWERS

CURRENT EVENTS   **274.** ▶ "No negotiations, no recognition, no peace."

ARTS & CULTURES   **275.** ▶ Sholom Aleichem.

PEOPLE   **276.** ▶ The first woman president of a major Hollywood movie studio.

RELIGION   **277.** ▶ Noah's Ark (Genesis) and the ark in which Moses floated down the Nile.

HISTORY   **278.** ▶ The invasion of Palestine by the German army of Field Marshal Rommel.

LANGUAGE   **279.** ▶ *Daven*.

GEOGRAPHY   **280.** ▶ Argentina.

CURRENT
EVENTS

281. ► What is the valley in Southwestern Lebanon occupied by Syrian forces in 1984 . . .?

ARTS &
CULTURES

282. ► This Jewish author wrote the novel *Exodus*, about the formation of Israel . . .?

PEOPLE

283. ► Which of King David's sons attempted to win the kingdom from his father in battle, but was killed while doing so?

RELIGION

284. ► By what means did Haman select the 13th of Adar as the day to destroy the Jews?

HISTORY

285. ► The German government expelled its Jewish residents 5 times since the 1300's. What were the years of these expulsions?

LANGUAGE

286. ► The Yiddish term *nachas* refers to . . .?

GEOGRAPHY

287. ► What country is northwest of Israel?

ANSWERS

CURRENT
EVENTS 281. ▶ The Bekaa Valley.

ARTS &
CULTURES 282. ▶ Leon Uris.

PEOPLE 283. ▶ Absalom (David's favorite son).

RELIGION 284. ▶ By the casting of lots. (Similar to drawing straws.)

HISTORY 285. ▶ 1388, 1416, 1439, 1614, and 1648 (This does not include the 20th century, in which Jews were not given a chance to leave).

LANGUAGE 286. ▶ A parent's happiness from seeing their children reach adulthood.

GEOGRAPHY 287. ▶ Syria.

CURRENT
EVENTS

288. ► The "Black Jews" of this country face persecution under a Marxist military regime, in the 1980's...?

ARTS &
CULTURES

289. ► Who wrote the well-known works on Jewish life, *World of Our Fathers* and *How We Lived*?

PEOPLE

290. ► This famous Jewish scholar and Talmudic interpreter taught the following concept: "In a place where there are no men, strive to be a man"...?

RELIGION

291. ► On which day, following the birth of a male child, should the *Bris*, or circumcision, take place?

HISTORY

292. ► The first instance in which the Jewish population was forced to wear a "Yellow Badge of Shame" occurred by this decree...?

LANGUAGE

293. ► It's a *Kipah* in Hebrew, but what is it in Yiddish?

GEOGRAPHY

294. ► Some descendants of the Marranos escaped to this country to avoid Spanish persecution, but were not allowed to openly avow their Jewish religion until 1910...?

ANSWERS

288. ▶ **Ethiopia.**

289. ▶ **Irving Howe.**

290. ▶ **Hillel.**

291. ▶ **The eighth day.**

292. ▶ **In 1215, the pope issued a degree forc-
ing Jews to wear yellow badges when
they left their ghettos, so that Christians could identify them.**

293. ▶ **Yarmulka.**

294. ▶ **Mexico.**

CURRENT
EVENTS

295. ► This man, known as the "Butcher of Lyon," was recently deported from Bolivia to France, to face war crimes charges . . .?

ARTS &
CULTURES

296. ► This Jewish female columnist is best known for her defense of the liberal view during the old Point-Counterpoint segment of the "Sixty Minutes" T.V. show . . .?

PEOPLE

297. ► This well known theologian of the Middle Ages said: "It is just as possible to convert the Jews as to convert the Devil" . . .?

RELIGION

298. ► How many Biblical Commandments, or *Mitzvot*, are there in Jewish Law?

HISTORY

299. ► When was the peak period of Jewish population throughout history?

LANGUAGE

300. ► The Yiddish expression for being drunk is . . .?

GEOGRAPHY

301. ► What country is southwest of Israel?

ANSWERS

295. ► Klaus Barbie.

296. ► Shana Alexander.

297. ► Martin Luther.

298. ► 613.

299. ► In the period preceding the Holocaust.

300. ► *Shikker*.

301. ► Egypt.

CURRENT
EVENTS

302. ► This Jewish lawyer led the Major League baseball players out on strike against the team owners . . .?

ARTS &
CULTURES

303. ► Why do charitable donations from Jewish sources often come in multiples of 18?

PEOPLE

304. ► These historic figures had one main thing in common: Mohammed, Pobjedonostew and Torquemada. . .?

RELIGION

305. ► In the 18th century, a new movement sprang up which advocated the spirituality of worship and considered Rabbis to be intermediaries of God. . .?

HISTORY

306. ► What was the "House of Bondage"?

LANGUAGE

307. ► The Yiddish expression *shiddach* means. . .?

GEOGRAPHY

308. ► What hill rises behind the city of Haifa. . .?

ANSWERS

CURRENT
EVENTS   302. ► Marvin Miller.

ARTS &
CULTURES   303. ► Eighteen in Hebrew letters spells *chai*, meaning "life." Thus, gifts in this multiple are considered "gifts of life."

PEOPLE   304. ► Hatred for the Jewish people.

RELIGION   305. ► Hassidism.

HISTORY   306. ► Egypt.

LANGUAGE   307. ► A social match.

GEOGRAPHY   308. ► Mount Carmel.

CURRENT
EVENTS

309. ► What is the symbol of peace on the emblem of Israel?

ARTS &
CULTURES

310. ► This Jewish New York theater personality is well known for his productions of "Shakespeare in the Park"...?

PEOPLE

311. ► Joyce Bauer, M.D., is known to millions of Americans by what professional name?

RELIGION

312. ► The "Days of Awe" refer to...?

HISTORY

313. ► In 1654, the first Jewish community in America was founded in which city?

LANGUAGE

314. ► The Yiddish expression *Zei gezunt* means...?

GEOGRAPHY

315. ► This is the only part of the Second Temple still existing...?

ANSWERS

CURRENT
EVENTS
309. ▶ **The olive branch.**

ARTS &
CULTURES
310. ▶ **Joseph Papp.**

PEOPLE
311. ▶ **Dr. Joyce Brothers.**

RELIGION
312. ▶ **The ten days from Rosh Hashanah to Yom Kippur.**

HISTORY
313. ▶ **New York (originally named New Amsterdam).**

LANGUAGE
314. ▶ **Be healthy.**

GEOGRAPHY
315. ▶ **The Western Wall or the Wailing Wall.**

CURRENT
EVENTS

316. ► Who is the present ruler of Jordan?

ARTS &
CULTURES

317. ► This Jewish film maker directed *2001, A Space Odyssey, Barry Lyndon* and *A Clockwork Orange*...?

PEOPLE

318. ► In 1917, the lobbying efforts of this British Jew were instrumental in the passage of the "Balfour Resolution"...?

RELIGION

319. ► The *Zohar* is the noted book of what group?

HISTORY

320. ► What mineral was mined from the Dead Sea in ancient times, and used by the Greeks in construction...?

LANGUAGE

321. ► *Har Hazikaron* is the location of a memorial to Holocaust victims. This translates to...?

GEOGRAPHY

322. ► What seas are connected by the Suez Canal?

ANSWERS

CURRENT
EVENTS

316. ► **King Hussein.**

ARTS &
CULTURES

317. ► **Stanley Kubrick.**

PEOPLE

318. ► **Chaim Weizman.**

RELIGION

319. ► **The Kabbalists.**

HISTORY

320. ► **Asphalt.**

LANGUAGE

321. ► **"Mount of Remembrance."**

GEOGRAPHY

322. ► **The Mediterranean is connected to the
Red Sea.**

CURRENT EVENTS
323. ► What was the Israeli government's name for the invasion of Lebanon?

ARTS & CULTURES
324. ► This Jewish opera singer is well known to baseball fans for his rendition of the national anthem, at Yankee Stadium...?

PEOPLE
325. ► This man is the foremost modern Hebrew author and won the Nobel Prize for Literature in 1966, the first Israeli to do so...?

RELIGION
326. ► What concept of final punishment was introduced by Christianity and is unknown to Judaism?

HISTORY
327. ► What was the name of the first daily Jewish newspaper founded in New York, on April 22, 1897...?

LANGUAGE
328. ► What does the name of the airline of Israel, "El Al," mean in Hebrew?

GEOGRAPHY
329. ► These two Biblical cities were located on the shores of the Dead Sea...?

ANSWERS

CURRENT EVENTS

323. ► Operation "Peace for Galilee."

ARTS & CULTURES

324. ► Robert Merrill.

PEOPLE

325. ► Shmuel Yosef Agnon.

RELIGION

326. ► Hell and Eternal Damnation.

HISTORY

327. ► The Jewish Daily Forward.

LANGUAGE

328. ► "Up in the air."

GEOGRAPHY

329. ► Sodom and Gomorrah.

CURRENT
EVENTS

330. ► Name one of the two camps outside of Beirut, where Christian militia men massacred Palestinian refugees...?

ARTS &
CULTURES

331. ► This Jewish actor was best known for his portrayal of the scion of T.V.'s Cartwright family...?

PEOPLE

332. ► He was the Commander of the Israeli Army during the Six-Day War and also served as Ambassador to the U.S....?

RELIGION

333. ► In ancient Israel, what were the responsibilities of the Levites?

HISTORY

334. ► The date 586 B.C.E. is significant in Jewish history. What happened to the Jews in Jerusalem on that date and where did some relocate to?

LANGUAGE

335. ► The Yiddish expressions: *Mazel Tov, L'Chaim* and *genig* mean...?

GEOGRAPHY

336. ► What are the four holiest cities in the Jewish religion?

ANSWERS

CURRENT
EVENTS

330. ► **Sabra or Shatila.**

ARTS &
CULTURES

331. ► **Lorne Green.**

PEOPLE

332. ► **Yitzchak Rabin.**

RELIGION

333. ► **Keepers of the Temple, judges and teachers.**

HISTORY

334. ► **Many were killed and the rest were exiled to Babylonia.**

LANGUAGE

335. ► **"Good luck," "to life" and "enough."**

GEOGRAPHY

336. ► **Hebron, Safed, Tiberias, and Jerusalem.**

CURRENT
EVENTS   337. ► Who is the current President of Syria?

ARTS &
CULTURES   338. ► This Jewish musician is one of the best
              known jazz flutists, with numerous
              albums to his credit...?

PEOPLE   339. ► He was the first Prime Minister of
              Israel...?

RELIGION   340. ► These time references: C.E. and B.C.E.
              mean...?

HISTORY   341. ► Founded in 1843, by Henry Jonas, it
              was the first Jewish service organiza-
              tion in America...?

LANGUAGE   342. ► The national anthem of Israel is
              "Hatikvah" and it means...?

GEOGRAPHY   343. ► The main geographic claim to fame of
              the Dead Sea is...?

ANSWERS

CURRENT
EVENTS   337. ► Hafez el Assad.

ARTS &
CULTURES   338. ► Herbie Mann.

PEOPLE   339. ► David Ben Gurion.

RELIGION   340. ► The "Common Era" and "Before the
                     Common Era."

HISTORY   341. ► B'nai B'rith.

LANGUAGE   342. ► The Hope.

GEOGRAPHY   343. ► Its shore is the lowest dry land in the
                     world.

CURRENT
EVENTS
344. ► Who succeeded Anwar Sadat as President of Egypt?

ARTS &
CULTURES
345. ► This Jewish performer was half of the biggest pop duo of the 1960's and then moved to acting, with a leading role in the hit movie *Carnal Knowledge*...?

PEOPLE
346. ► Who is known as the father of modern Hebrew?

RELIGION
347. ► Reform Judaism originated where and when?

HISTORY
348. ► How did God punish Pharaoh's daughter for speaking against Moses?

LANGUAGE
349. ► These Yiddish expressions: to *Kvell* and to *Kvetch* refer to...?

GEOGRAPHY
350. ► It has been proposed that these two bodies of water be connected by a major Israeli hydro-electric project...?

ANSWERS

344. ▶ Husni Mubarak.

345. ▶ Art Garfunkel.

346. ▶ Eliezer Ben-Yehuda.

347. ▶ Germany, in the early 1800's.

348. ▶ With leprosy.

349. ▶ Being "proud" and being a "complainer."

350. ▶ The Mediterranean and the Dead Sea.

CURRENT
EVENTS

351. ► What is the *Hidon Ha'Tanach*, held in Israel each year?

ARTS &
CULTURES

352. ► This Jewish author wrote the book *Making It* and is the editor of the magazine *Commentary*...?

PEOPLE

353. ► She was the first female in history elected as a head of State...?

RELIGION

354. ► A Jewish girl becomes *Bat Mitzvah* at this age...?

HISTORY

355. ► What French monarch began the emancipation of the Jews?

LANGUAGE

356. ► This is the official second language of Israel...?

GEOGRAPHY

357. ► In 1948, the Hebrew term *Kibbutz Galuyot* became a major principle of Israel's Declaration of Independence. It means...?

ANSWERS

351. ► Contests of Bible knowledge.

352. ► Norman Podhoretz.

353. ► Golda Meir.

354. ► Twelve.

355. ► Napoleon.

356. ► Arabic.

357. ► Ingathering of the Exiles.

CURRENT EVENTS

358. ► This Jewish U.S. Admiral launched the world's first atomic-powered submarine...?

ARTS & CULTURES

359. ► What Jewish songwriter and political activist was immortalized in the movie *Bound for Glory*?

PEOPLE

360. ► This Jewish athlete won gold and silver medals at the Paris Olympics of 1924, and was the subject of the movie *Chariots of Fire*?

RELIGION

361. ► What is the ancient Hebrew name for a marriage contract?

HISTORY

362. ► Which empire assumed control of Palestine after the collapse of the Roman Empire?

LANGUAGE

363. ► The six-sided Jewish Star is commonly known in Hebrew as...?

GEOGRAPHY

364. ► What ancient city is located on the Sea of Galilee?

ANSWERS

CURRENT
EVENTS   358. ► **Admiral Hyman Rickover (tireless advocate of the nuclear-powered navy).**

ARTS &
CULTURES   359. ► **Woody Guthrie.**

PEOPLE   360. ► **Harold Abrahams.**

RELIGION   361. ► *Ketubah.*

HISTORY   362. ► **The Byzantine Empire.**

LANGUAGE   363. ► **The "Magen David" (the Shield of David).**

GEOGRAPHY   364. ► **Tiberias.**

CURRENT EVENTS

365. ► After the invasion of Lebanon this President-elect was murdered by a bomb blast in his office. Who was he?

ARTS & CULTURES

366. ► This Jewish actor is well known for his role as Sonny Corleone in *The God-father...?*

PEOPLE

367. ► Element number 99 is named for this famous Jewish physicist...?

RELIGION

368. ► What Biblical figure does the women's group Hadassah take its name from?

HISTORY

369. ► This Biblical character came from the land of Uz...?

LANGUAGE

370. ► The Hebrew word *knesset* translates into...?

GEOGRAPHY

371. ► These four countries border Israel...?

ANSWERS

365. ► Bashir Gemayel.

366. ► James Caan.

367. ► Albert Einstein.

368. ► Ruth (Hadassah is the Hebrew form of
the Persian name Ruth).

369. ► Job.

370. ► Assembly.

371. ► Lebanon, Syria, Jordan, Egypt.

CURRENT EVENTS

372. ► What position did Chaim Bar-Lev have in the 1968 and 1969 Israeli government led by Golda Meir?

ARTS & CULTURES

373. ► What do Nelly Sachs and Shmuel Yosef Agnon have in common?

PEOPLE

374. ► This Jewish born thinker founded socialism...?

RELIGION

375. ► It is customary for the Jewish people to face this direction during prayer...?

HISTORY

376. ► In modern times, what law or act first recognized the Jewish right to a homeland in Palestine?

LANGUAGE

377. ► This term refers to the countries outside of Israel where Jews reside...?

GEOGRAPHY

378. ► Egypt blockaded Israeli shipping here, in the days preceding the Six-Day War of 1967...?

ANSWERS

372. ► **Commander-in-chief.**

373. ► **These Jewish writers shared the Nobel Prize for literature in 1966.**

374. ► **Karl Marx.**

375. ► **East.**

376. ► **The Balfour Declaration.**

377. ► **The Diaspora.**

378. ► **Sharm el Sheik or the Straits of Tiran.**

CURRENT
EVENTS

379. ► The infamous plane hijacking to Entebbe, Uganda took place on what airline?

ARTS &
CULTURES

380. ► Why is it likely that William Shakespeare had never in his life seen a Jew when he wrote *The Merchant of Venice?*

PEOPLE

381. ► These Jewish financiers were the first to popularize the making of loans to nations...?

RELIGION

382. ► The word written on the back of a *mezuzah* is...?

HISTORY

383. ► Most Jews, during the Middle Ages, did not go into agriculture because of these restrictions...?

LANGUAGE

384. ► This popular Yiddish expression refers to a beggar or an extremely cheap person...?

GEOGRAPHY

385. ► Herod's Fortress was otherwise known as...?

ANSWERS

CURRENT
EVENTS   379. ► Air France.

ARTS &
CULTURES   380. ► Because the Jews of England had been
                     expelled at that time (in 1290).

PEOPLE   381. ► The Rothschilds.

RELIGION   382. ► *Shaddai* ("Almighty").

HISTORY   383. ► The prohibition against Jews owning
                     land.

LANGUAGE   384. ► *Shnorrer*.

GEOGRAPHY   385. ► Masada.

CURRENT
EVENTS   386. ► Which group of people recently discovered the Dead Sea Scrolls and sold them to the Israelis?

ARTS &
CULTURES   387. ► Who was Adolph Zukor?

PEOPLE   388. ► The prayer for the sanctification of wine is called...?

RELIGION   389. ► What caused Haman to attempt to murder the Jews?

HISTORY   390. ► This book of the Bible tells the Story of Creation...?

LANGUAGE   391. ► Who were the Christians who controlled Palestine in the Middle Ages?

GEOGRAPHY   392. ► This range of hills divides Israel and Syria...?

ANSWERS

CURRENT EVENTS 386. ► **The Bedouins.**

ARTS & CULTURES 387. ► **The movie mogul (who controlled Paramount Studios for 40 years).**

PEOPLE 388. ► **The *Kiddish*.**

RELIGION 389. ► **He was angry because a Jew would not bow down to him.**

HISTORY 390. ► **Genesis.**

LANGUAGE 391. ► **The Crusaders.**

GEOGRAPHY 392. ► **Golan Heights.**

CURRENT
EVENTS

393. ► How many official languages does Israel have and what are they?

ARTS &
CULTURES

394. ► The clothing article known as a *streimel* is...?

PEOPLE

395. ► In 1906, Oscar Straus became the first Jew in America to hold this position...?

RELIGION

396. ► What is the Touro Synagogue noted for?

HISTORY

397. ► In the late 16th century, in what 2 sympathetic countries did Jews find hope for a peaceful and better life?

LANGUAGE

398. ► These Yiddish expressions: *mensch* and *meshiggener* refer to...?

GEOGRAPHY

399. ► On *Hanukah*, this item is transported from Modiin to Jerusalem...?

ANSWERS

CURRENT
EVENTS 393. ► Two: Hebrew and Arabic.

ARTS &
CULTURES 394. ► A fur-trimmed hat worn by some Hassidim.

PEOPLE 395. ► He became the first U.S. Cabinet member when Theodore Roosevelt appointed him Secretary of Commerce and Labor.

RELIGION 396. ► It is the oldest synagogue in America.

HISTORY 397. ► Holland and Denmark. (From this time until the Nazi era, the Jews thrived in this region. Even during the Nazi era these governments did not comply with German orders to round up their Jewish populations for deportation.)

LANGUAGE 398. ► A good, well-meaning person and a crazy person.

GEOGRAPHY 399. ► A torch.

CURRENT
EVENTS

400. ► In 1979, this official in the Carter administration held an unauthorized meeting with P.L.O. observers to the U.N. which later caused his resignation...?

ARTS &
CULTURES

401. ► This renowned Jewish resort area, in the Catskills mountain area of New York State, is known in the entertainment industry as...?

PEOPLE

402. ► This man, known as the "Nazi Hunter," has a center for Holocaust studies named after him...?

RELIGION

403. ► The one week mourning period following the death of a relative is called...?

HISTORY

404. ► This tribunal persecuted Jews in Medieval Spain...?

LANGUAGE

405. ► What does the word *Ben*, frequently appearing in Jewish names, mean?

GEOGRAPHY

406. ► In 73 C.E., Zealots defending this fortress chose death rather than face capture and slavery?

ANSWERS

CURRENT
EVENTS

400. ▶ **Andrew Young.**

ARTS &
CULTURES

401. ▶ **The "Borscht Belt".**

PEOPLE

402. ▶ **Simon Wiesenthal.**

RELIGION

403. ▶ *Shiva.*

HISTORY

404. ▶ **The Inquisition.**

LANGUAGE

405. ▶ **"Son of".**

GEOGRAPHY

406. ▶ **Masada.**

CURRENT
EVENTS

407. ► This Jewish organization uses as its symbol a fist inside of a Star of David...?

ARTS &
CULTURES

408. ► Jewish dancer Murray Teichman is a hero to people who can't coordinate their feet with the music. He is known as...?

PEOPLE

409. ► Israel Beer Josaphat changed his Jewish name to get into journalism and later created this major news agency that bore his new name...?

RELIGION

410. ► The image of the dove carrying an olive branch is related to this story in the Bible...?

HISTORY

411. ► He built the First Temple.

LANGUAGE

412. ► What does *Golem* refer to?

GEOGRAPHY

413. ► What industry is located at the southern end of the Dead Sea?

ANSWERS

CURRENT
EVENTS **407.** ► **The Jewish Defense League.**

ARTS &
CULTURES **408.** ► **Arthur Murray.**

PEOPLE **409.** ► **Reuters.**

RELIGION **410.** ► **The Flood.**

HISTORY **411.** ► **King Solomon.**

LANGUAGE **412.** ► **A creation of man that is given life
through magical means.**

GEOGRAPHY **413.** ► **Salt and chemical extraction.**

CURRENT
EVENTS

414. ► Who were the joint recipients of the 1978 Nobel Peace Prize?

ARTS &
CULTURES

415. ► Jewish comedian Milton Sills holds the world's record for being hit in the face with cream pies. What is his show business name?

PEOPLE

416. ► Milwaukee was the childhood home of this notable Israeli leader...?

RELIGION

417. ► The *Haggadah* relates events occurring in which book of the Bible...?

HISTORY

418. ► The State of Israel was proclaimed in this month of this year...?

LANGUAGE

419. ► The Yiddish exclamation *Gevalt* means?

GEOGRAPHY

420. ► What is the only fresh water lake in Israel today?

ANSWERS

414. ► **Menachem Begin and Anwar Sadat.**

415. ► **Soupy Sales.**

416. ► **Golda Meir.**

417. ► **Exodus.**

418. ► **May, 1948.**

419. ► **Help.**

420. ► **The Sea of Galilee.**

CURRENT EVENTS
421. ► What percent of world Jewry lives in Israel?

ARTS & CULTURES
422. ► These Jewish women, Anna Pavlova and Alicia Markova, have this in common...?

PEOPLE
423. ► This Russian writer and participant in the Russian Revolution was born Lev Davidovich Bronstein, but is better known by his pen name...?

RELIGION
424. ► Why do some Passover observers leave an empty chair at the Passover Seder table?

HISTORY
425. ► A *shofar* can be made from the horn of any kosher animal except the cow or the ox. What is the important symbolic reasoning behind this exclusion?

LANGUAGE
426. ► The English root of the word *Talmud* is...?

GEOGRAPHY
427. ► What ancient land was known for its beautiful cedar trees?

ANSWERS

CURRENT EVENTS 421. ► Twenty percent.

ARTS & CULTURES 422. ► Both were famous ballerinas.

PEOPLE 423. ► Leon Trotsky.

RELIGION 424. ► To show a symbolic solidarity with fellow Jews from the Soviet Union who cannot freely celebrate the holiday.

HISTORY 425. ► Using the horns of cows and oxen would remind the Jewish people of their greatest transgression—the constructing of the Golden Calf in the Sinai. Therefore, this would be symbolically inappropriate.

LANGUAGE 426. ► To learn.

GEOGRAPHY 427. ► Lebanon.

CURRENT
EVENTS   428. ► The "Law of Return" states...?

ARTS &
CULTURES   429. ► This famous Jewish artist designed the mosaics and tapestries inside the Israeli Knesset building...?

PEOPLE   430. ► He personally donated the largest amount of money in history, over $45,000,000, to resettle the abused Jews of Russia in other countries...?

RELIGION   431. ► The story of Genesis ends with G-d's creation of...?

HISTORY   432. ► In the Bible, whose family had 12 sons and one daughter?

LANGUAGE   433. ► What did the "San Remo Conference" of 1920 ratify?

GEOGRAPHY   434. ► The popular Hebrew word for immigration is...?

ANSWERS

CURRENT
EVENTS

428. ► Any Jew who settles in Israel is immediately granted citizenship upon request.

ARTS &
CULTURES

429. ► Marc Chagall.

PEOPLE

430. ► Baron Maurice de Hirsch.

RELIGION

431. ► Man.

HISTORY

432. ► Jacob's.

LANGUAGE

433. ► The Balfour Declaration (it also awarded the Mandate for Palestine to Great Britain).

GEOGRAPHY

434. ► *Aliyah.*

CURRENT
EVENTS   435. ► What Palestinian group was Yasir
                Arafat the leader of, before he as-
                sumed leadership of the entire P.L.O.,
                in 1970?

ARTS &
CULTURES   436. ► What do these three companies have
                in common: Kedem, Monarch, and
                Carmel?

PEOPLE   437. ► Bernard M. Baruch, the Jewish finan-
                cier, held what powerful government
                post during World War II?

RELIGION   438. ► What are *peyot*?

HISTORY   439. ► What were the weapons used by
                David and the weapons used by
                Goliath in their famous battle?

LANGUAGE   440. ► *Kiddish* means...?

GEOGRAPHY   441. ► This is Israel's main Seaport...?

ANSWERS

435. ► *El-Fatah*.

436. ► They are all kosher wine manu-
facturers.

437. ► Chairman of the War Industries
Board.

438. ► Side locks worn by Orthodox Jews.

439. ► David used a sling and a stone, and
Goliath used a spear and a javelin.

440. ► Sanctification.

441. ► Haifa.

CURRENT
EVENTS

442. ► The seal of the State of Israel is represented by these two symbolic items...?

ARTS &
CULTURES

443. ► This Jewish entertainer is dubbed "The Divine Miss M"...?

PEOPLE

444. ► Who commanded the Jews on Masada?

RELIGION

445. ► When Moses received the Ten Commandments what was the weather condition?

HISTORY

446. ► Who are the four sons mentioned in the Passover Haggadah?

LANGUAGE

447. ► What was the dilemma the Jewish settlers in Palestine faced in their decision to join the British in fighting the Nazis?

GEOGRAPHY

448. ► What does the word *Judesmo* refer to?

ANSWERS

CURRENT
EVENTS

442. ► A Menorah (representing the enlightenment of culture) and leaves (representing fruitfulness and peace).

ARTS &
CULTURES

443. ► Bette Midler.

PEOPLE

444. ► Eleazar ben Yair.

RELIGION

445. ► Thunder and lightning.

HISTORY

446. ► The wise son, the wicked son, the simple son and the son who does not know to ask.

LANGUAGE

447. ► The Jews were fighting the British for greater rights and freedoms at the same time they agreed to help the British fight the Nazis.

GEOGRAPHY

448. ► The Sephardic language—a synonym for Ladino.

CURRENT
EVENTS

449. ► This Jewish Congressman from New York and long time loyal ally of Israel lost his battle with cancer in 1982...?

ARTS &
CULTURES

450. ► This Jewish writer wrote the science fiction book *Foundation's Edge*...?

PEOPLE

451. ► These men: Solomon, Absalom and Adonijah, are his sons...?

RELIGION

452. ► On Purim, celebrants are permitted to drink so much that they cannot distinguish between these two Purim characters...?

HISTORY

453. ► After the suppression of Bar Kochba's government by the Romans, Jewish independence was over for how many years?

LANGUAGE

454. ► What is the literal and seldom used translation of the Hebrew word *goy*?

GEOGRAPHY

455. ► What was the first country that the ancient Jews were foreigners in?

ANSWERS

CURRENT
EVENTS   **449.** ► **Benjamin Rosenthal (Democrat from NY).**

ARTS &
CULTURES   **450.** ► **Isaac Asimov.**

PEOPLE   **451.** ► **David.**

RELIGION   **452.** ► **Mordechai and Haman.**

HISTORY   **453.** ► **More than 1800 years.**

LANGUAGE   **454.** ► **Nation.**

GEOGRAPHY   **455.** ► **Egypt.**

CURRENT EVENTS

456. ► What was the Israeli response to the "Fez Plan," presented in 1982 by the Arab League?

ARTS & CULTURES

457. ► This Jewish author and resident of Jerusalem received the Nobel Prize for Literature in 1966...?

PEOPLE

458. ► The Friedman sisters are otherwise known by their famous newspaper advice column names...?

RELIGION

459. ► What three procedures are mandatory at every conversion to Judaism?

HISTORY

460. ► Solomon's Palace took how many years to build?

LANGUAGE

461. ► A *Cheder* refers to...?

GEOGRAPHY

462. ► These two Biblical cities are symbols of evil...?

ANSWERS

456. ► They rejected it because it deviated from the Camp David agreements and they viewed it as a veiled "declaration of war."

457. ► S.Y. Agnon.

458. ► Ann Landers and Abigail Van Buren.

459. ► Candidates must request conversion on their own; take instruction in Judaism; and attempts to dissuade candidates must be made.

460. ► Thirteen.

461. ► A Jewish school (in Eastern Europe until World War II).

462. ► Sodom and Gomorrah.

CURRENT
EVENTS

463. ► This man and his organization introduced the slogan "Never Again," which meant that his followers would fight anyone thought to be an enemy or that professed anti-Semitism...?

ARTS &
CULTURES

464. ► This Jewish composer wrote the music to Broadway's *A Chorus Line*...?

PEOPLE

465. ► What position were both Jeroboam and Rehoboam noted for?

RELIGION

466. ► This Biblical figure dreamt of seven fat and seven lean cows...?

HISTORY

467. ► Where was the main center of the Jewish community located, between the years 1000 B.C.E. and 200 B.C.E.?

LANGUAGE

468. ► This seldom used anti-Semitic reference to a geographic location was popularized by a candidate in the 1984 Presidential election. Where is "Hymie-Town"?

GEOGRAPHY

469. ► The story of *Fiddler on the Roof* occurs in this little town...?

ANSWERS

463. ► Meir Kahane and the Jewish Defense League.

464. ► Marvin Hamlisch.

465. ► They were Kings of Israel (after Solomon). (Kings I.)

466. ► Pharaoh.

467. ► Babylon.

468. ► It is New York City. (The Reverend Jesse Jackson later apologized for using this term.)

469. ► Anatevka.

CURRENT
EVENTS

470. ► Israel has both civil and religious courts. Which cases go before religious courts?

ARTS &
CULTURES

471. ► He wrote the classic modern work *History of the Jews...?*

PEOPLE

472. ► He modernized the Hebrew language.

RELIGION

473. ► What is symbolized by the two cups of wine at a wedding ceremony, that both the bride and groom drink from?

HISTORY

474. ► How long did it take King Solomon to build the First Temple?

LANGUAGE

475. ► The people of Israel had a slogan, *Kibbush Hashmama*, referring to the harsh environment. In English this means...?

GEOGRAPHY

476. ► The largest desert area in Israel is...?

ANSWERS

470. ▶ **Personal status cases, such as marriage, divorce, etc.**

471. ▶ **Heinrich Graetz.**

472. ▶ **Ben Yehuda.**

473. ▶ **The cups of joy and sorrow, demonstrating their willingness to remain together no matter what life may bring.**

474. ▶ **Seven years.**

475. ▶ **"The Conquest of the Desert."**

476. ▶ **The Negev.**

CURRENT
EVENTS

477. ► What event sparked the Christian Phalangist Massacre in Sabra and Shatila?

ARTS &
CULTURES

478. ► Which old-time Jewish comedian was born with the name Joseph Abramowitz?

PEOPLE

479. ► What was the most important post that Itzhak Ben-Zvi held in Israel?

RELIGION

480. ► What was the First Priests' main responsibility during the Jewish people's forty years of wandering in the desert?

HISTORY

481. ► What was the approximate world Jewish population in the 12th century?

LANGUAGE

482. ► In which person (or tense) are injunctions in the Bible usually worded?

GEOGRAPHY

483. ► *Bet Ha'Nasi* refers to which place in Israel?

ANSWERS

477. ► The assassination of Lebanese President-elect Bashir Gemayel.

478. ► Joey Adams.

479. ► President of Israel (twice, from 1952-1963).

480. ► To guard the Ark or the *Mishkan* that held the Ten Commandments.

481. ► A little more than one million.

482. ► The second person.

483. ► The President's residence in Jerusalem.

CURRENT
EVENTS

484. ► What controversial economic remedy did former Finance Minister of Israel, Yoram Aridor, suggest that resulted in his resignation?

ARTS &
CULTURES

485. ► This Jewish actor starred in a spin-off sitcom that developed from "The Mary Tyler Moore Show"...?

PEOPLE

486. ► This Jewish financier provided the funds for Columbus' voyage to America...?

RELIGION

487. ► The pious Jew will wear this when he says certain prayers...?

HISTORY

488. ► Name any four of the twelve tribes of Israel...?

LANGUAGE

489. ► What does *Ir Ha-Atika* refer to?

GEOGRAPHY

490. ► The city of Dimona is noted for this Israeli achievement...?

ANSWERS

CURRENT EVENTS

484. ▶ "Dollarizing" the Israeli economy (linking it directly to the U.S. dollar).

ARTS & CULTURES

485. ▶ Ed Asner (in "Lou Grant").

PEOPLE

486. ▶ Louis Santangel.

RELIGION

487. ▶ *Talith*.

HISTORY

488. ▶ (Any four of these): Levi, Benjamin, Simeon, Reuben, Naphtali, Judah, Zebulun, Gad, Dan, Issachar, Joseph and Asher.

LANGUAGE

489. ▶ The Old City of Jerusalem.

GEOGRAPHY

490. ▶ It is the home of Israel's first atomic reactor.

CURRENT
EVENTS

491. ► Tay-Sachs disease disrupts the functioning of which system of the human body, affecting Jews in higher proportions than gentiles?

ARTS &
CULTURES

492. ► This Jewish author wrote *Fear of Flying* and *How to Save Your Own Life*...?

PEOPLE

493. ► This Jewish teacher was the first to state the Golden Rule...?

RELIGION

494. ► The first person called up to read the Law in Orthodox services is...?

HISTORY

495. ► How long was the Jewish period of captivity in Babylon?

LANGUAGE

496. ► What does *Megillah* mean?

GEOGRAPHY

497. ► The legendary Tomb of King David is located here...?

ANSWERS

CURRENT EVENTS 491. ► The nervous system.

ARTS & CULTURES 492. ► Erica Jong.

PEOPLE 493. ► Hillel.

RELIGION 494. ► Either a Cohen or a member of the House of Aaron.

HISTORY 495. ► Forty-nine years.

LANGUAGE 496. ► Scroll.

GEOGRAPHY 497. ► Mount Zion, in Jerusalem.

CURRENT
EVENTS

498. ► The Israeli government is planning the introduction of this new defensive weapon in 1986. It will be produced in Israel and will be called the "Lavie". What is it?

ARTS &
CULTURES

499. ► This famous Jewish lyricist wrote the words for *West Side Story*...?

PEOPLE

500. ► Who was the famous Jewish historian who recorded the battles of the Romans and the Jews?

RELIGION

501. ► Who received an article of clothing from his father, making his other brothers very angry?

HISTORY

502. ► In the 16th century, Jewish leader Don Joseph Nassi, the first modern Zionist, attempted to create an independent state in Palestine. What city did he build a wall around, wanting it to become the capital?

LANGUAGE

503. ► What were the *Rishonim* and the *Aharonim*, as related to the Biblical prophets?

GEOGRAPHY

504. ► The tomb of Maimonides (or Rambam) is located in this Israeli lake region...?

ANSWERS

CURRENT EVENTS 498. ► A new supersonic jet fighter.

ARTS & CULTURES 499. ► Stephen Sondheim.

PEOPLE 500. ► Yosef ben Matatyahu, better known as Josephus Flavius (who had been one of the Jewish commanders in the Galilee and later switched his allegiance to the Romans).

RELIGION 501. ► Joseph received the coat of many colors from Jacob.

HISTORY 502. ► Tiberias.

LANGUAGE 503. ► *Rishonim* are the early prophets; *Aharonim* are the later prophets.

GEOGRAPHY 504. ► Tiberias.

CURRENT EVENTS
505. ► What was Israel's most daring military raid since their Entebbe hostage rescue?

ARTS & CULTURES
506. ► This Jewish author mainly writes and lectures about the Holocaust...?

PEOPLE
507. ► The Italian Jew, Ernesto Nathan, was the first Jew to hold what office, from 1907 to 1913?

RELIGION
508. ► Why is *Tefillin* placed on the head?

HISTORY
509. ► What was the first modern day Jewish agricultural settlement in Israel?

LANGUAGE
510. ► Where did the *Pentateuch* get its name?

GEOGRAPHY
511. ► The League of Nations made this momentous decision concerning Palestine, in 1919...?

ANSWERS

505. ► The destruction of Iraq's nuclear reactor (in Osiraq near Baghdad) on June 7, 1981.

ARTS & CULTURES 506. ► Elie Weisel.

PEOPLE 507. ► The mayor of Rome.

RELIGION 508. ► To remind the worshipper that one's actions, thoughts and desires are subject to the Law.

HISTORY 509. ► "Petach Tikvah."

LANGUAGE 510. ► From the Greek *pente* and *teuchos*, meaning "five books".

GEOGRAPHY 511. ► They approved of the British mandate to rule Palestine.

CURRENT
EVENTS

512. ► What does A.D.L. stand for?

ARTS &
CULTURES

513. ► Which Jewish swing band leader was born with the name Isaac Arshawsky?

PEOPLE

514. ► In 1880's Palestine, he was known as *Hanadiv Ha-Yaduah* or "The well-known Benefactor"...?

RELIGION

515. ► The first romance in the Bible was between...?

HISTORY

516. ► Who were Russia's Jewish "Cantonists"?

LANGUAGE

517. ► The name *Tel Aviv* was first mentioned here...?

GEOGRAPHY

518. ► This Gate of Jerusalem's Old City has the same name as an Israeli city...?

ANSWERS

CURRENT
EVENTS 512. ▶ Anti-Defamation League.

ARTS &
CULTURES 513. ▶ Artie Shaw.

PEOPLE 514. ▶ Baron Edmond de Rothschild (the French Philanthropist who supported the early settlements in Palestine).

RELIGION 515. ▶ Jacob and Rachel.

HISTORY 516. ▶ Young Jewish boys forcibly inducted into the Russian army.

LANGUAGE 517. ▶ In the Bible (a town in Babel inhabited by Judean refugees after the destruction of the First Temple).

GEOGRAPHY 518. ▶ Jaffa Gate.

CURRENT EVENTS

519. ► What position did Shimon Peres hold in the 1974 government of Israel?

ARTS & CULTURES

520. ► In 1979, what famous 1960's and 1970's Jewish folk and rock singer converted from Judaism to become a Christian?

PEOPLE

521. ► This Arab leader organized a German S.S.-style Moslem legion which played an active role in the German army and assisted in the killing of European Jews...?

RELIGION

522. ► This Prophet said: "Learn to do well, seek justice, relieve the oppressed, judge the fatherless, plead for the widow"...?

HISTORY

523. ► What was the "Peal Committee"?

LANGUAGE

524. ► These Hebrew names — *Ir HaEmel* and *Ir HaZedek* — refer to the same place, Jerusalem, although they mean different things. What do they mean?

GEOGRAPHY

525. ► In which direction does the Jordan River flow?

ANSWERS

CURRENT
EVENTS 519. ► Defense Minister.

ARTS &
CULTURES 520. ► Bob Dylan.

PEOPLE 521. ► The Mufti of Jersalem (Haj Amin al—
huseyni killed Jews in Yugoslavia,
Vilna and Kovna).

RELIGION 522. ► Isaiah.

HISTORY 523. ► A Royal Committee, which was the
first to recommend the partition of
Palestine into Arab and Jewish states.

LANGUAGE 524. ► *Ir HaEmet* means "City of Truth"; *Ir
HaZedek* means "City of Justice".

GEOGRAPHY 525. ► From north to south.

CURRENT
EVENTS

526. ► On November 10th, 1975 the U.N. passed this outrageous resolution...?

ARTS &
CULTURES

527. ► What famous New York-based Jewish and Irish husband and wife comedy team have worked together for more than two decades...?

PEOPLE

528. ► This French Jewish army Captain was unjustly convicted of treason, in 1895...?

RELIGION

529. ► Why is an animal designated *Nevela*, unfit for Jewish consumption?

HISTORY

530. ► What was the "Jewish Brigade"?

LANGUAGE

531. ► What does *synagogue* translate to in English?

GEOGRAPHY

532. ► This institution is located on Mount Scopus, overlooking Jerusalem?

ANSWERS

526. ► Condemning Zionism as a racist movement.

527. ► Jerry Stiller and Anne Meara.

528. ► Alfred Dreyfus.

529. ► Because it died a natural death (as opposed to being slaughtered).

530. ► A Jewish military unit within the British Army during World War II.

531. ► Place of assembly (derived from the Greek).

532. ► The Hebrew University.

CURRENT
EVENTS

533. ► This Jewish daily newspaper is the longest running Yiddish-language newspaper in the United States...?

ARTS &
CULTURES

534. ► This Jewish comedienne was known as Lisa Loopner and Roseanne Roseannadanna...?

PEOPLE

535. ► This Jewish scholar is a leading business economist and longtime confidante of Republican presidents, having served as the chairman of the Council of Economic Advisors...?

RELIGION

536. ► The two Biblically significant occurrences on the mountain "Moriah", are...?

HISTORY

537. ► These temporary identifying marks were required of all Jews by the Nazis...?

LANGUAGE

538. ► Name the Hebrew months...?

GEOGRAPHY

539. ► The four ancient holy cities are...?

ANSWERS

533. ► *The Jewish Daily Forward.*

534. ► **Gilda Radner.**

535. ► **Alan Greenspan.**

536. ► **It was the mountain that the Temple was built on, and upon which G-d tested Abraham.**

537. ► **Yellow Stars of David pinned to their clothing.**

538. ► **Tishre, Heshvan, Kislev, Tebeth, Shebat, Adar, Nisan, Iyar, Sivan, Tammuz, Ab, Elul.**

539. ► **Jerusalem, Hebron, Safed and Tiberias.**

CURRENT
EVENTS

540. ► Who said, between 1976 and 1980, "There's a hell of a lot more Arabs than there is Jews" and "The Jewish media tears up the Arab countries full time"...?

ARTS &
CULTURES

541. ► This Jewish singer made famous the song "Oh My Papa", and also wrote an autobiography...?

PEOPLE

542. ► This Jewish family owns the richest Jewish oil fortune in the world...?

RELIGION

543. ► This Biblical book is the easiest to take quotations from...?

HISTORY

544. ► The Sinai Campaign occurred in this year...?

LANGUAGE

545. ► What is the *Yetzer tov* and the *Yetzer rah*?

GEOGRAPHY

546. ► The Jewish quarter of what city is known as the Marais?

ANSWERS

CURRENT
EVENTS 540. ▶ Billy Carter.

ARTS &
CULTURES 541. ▶ Eddie Fischer.

PEOPLE 542. ▶ The Marvin Davis family.

RELIGION 543. ▶ Proverbs.

HISTORY 544. ▶ 1956.

LANGUAGE 545. ▶ The good inclination and the bad inclination. (Judaism believes that people are born with both and life is a struggle to overcome one with the other.)

GEOGRAPHY 546. ▶ Paris.

CURRENT
EVENTS

547. ▶ President Carter made this shocking and inconsistent comment referring to the Palestinians, in 1977...?

ARTS &
CULTURES

548. ▶ This Jewish professor, astronomer and author is also an actor on his own T.V. series...?

PEOPLE

549. ▶ This Canadian Jewish family may be the richest in the world and they made it through real estate...?

RELIGION

550. ▶ Who was the first *kohen* or priest?

HISTORY

551. ▶ This Syrian-Greek leader desecrated the Temple...?

LANGUAGE

552. ▶ The Yiddish word *Shaytl* means...?

GEOGRAPHY

553. ▶ After the exile of the Jews and the decline of Babylon, where was the next great center of Jewish learning, outside of Israel?

ANSWERS

547. ► He called for a "homeland" for Palestinians.

548. ► Dr. Carl Sagan ("Cosmos").

549. ► The Reichman family.

550. ► Aaron (Moses' brother).

551. ► Antiochus Epiphanes. (He tried to put an end to Jewish cultural life.)

552. ► A wig.

553. ► Spain (in the late ninth century this became the emerging area for Jewish life and learning in the world.)

Trivia Judaica™   QUESTIONS

CURRENT
EVENTS

554. ► How did the International Soccer Federation react to the banning of Israel from the 1976 Asian Games?

ARTS &
CULTURES

555. ► These 5 American Jewish leaders all had something in common: Benjamin Jonas, Simon Guggenheim, Joseph Simon, Isidore Ragnor, David Levy...?

PEOPLE

556. ► This notorious war criminal was tried in Jerusalem, in 1961...?

RELIGION

557. ► What are the three cardinal sins?

HISTORY

558. ► The destruction of Jewish stores and Synagogues and the random murder of Jews in 1938 Germany, was later referred to as...?

LANGUAGE

559. ► A *Chazzen* is Yiddish for this occupation...?

GEOGRAPHY

560. ► In Israel, what is 120 miles long and known as the *Araveh*?

ANSWERS

554. ► They rejected the ban and Israel participated.

555. ► They were all United States senators.

556. ► Adolph Eichmann.

557. ► Idolatry, murder and adultery.

558. ► *Kristallnacht* or "The Night of Broken Glass".

559. ► A cantor.

560. ► It is a great plain stretching from the Dead Sea to Eilat. It borders the Negev and the Mountains of Jordan.

CURRENT
EVENTS

561. ► What action did France take against the organizer of the Munich Olympic massacre, after he was arrested in Paris, in 1976?

ARTS &
CULTURES

562. ► This French Jewish woman is the owner of a chic world-wide chain of discos...?

PEOPLE

563. ► This Jewish author broke the *My Lai Massacre* story and also wrote a recent scathing book about Henry Kissinger...?

RELIGION

564. ► Why was the two-volume "Book of the Maccabees", including the story of Chanukah, not included in the Bible?

HISTORY

565. ► What document is the following quote taken from: "The British Government views with favor the establishment in Palestine of a national home for the Jewish people..."?

LANGUAGE

566. ► What is the rare action known as a *Herem*?

GEOGRAPHY

567. ► Jericho is one of the most historically important cities in the world for this very unique reason...?

ANSWERS

561. ▶ They released him.

562. ▶ Regine Choukroun (Regine's Disco-
theque).

563. ▶ Seymour Hersh.

564. ▶ Because they glorified war and other
non-Jewish influences (and were instead included in the Apocrypha).

565. ▶ The Balfour Declaration (November 2,
1917).

566. ▶ An excommunication from Judaism
for heresy or for violations of Jewish
law. (A *herem* was once called against
the radical philosopher Spinoza.)

567. ▶ It is the oldest city in the world (over
10,000 years old).

CURRENT
EVENTS   568. ▶ What was Israel's daring "Operation Babylon"?

ARTS &
CULTURES   569. ▶ What was Jewish writer Neil Simon's most successful play?

PEOPLE   570. ▶ This famous Zionist said: "Either you liquidate the Diaspora or the Diaspora will liquidate you"...?

RELIGION   571. ▶ A period of approximately how many years is covered in the Bible?

HISTORY   572. ▶ This leading world power (at the time) was responsible for the destruction of the Second Temple in 70 C.E....?

LANGUAGE   573. ▶ What do the words on a traditional Chanukah dreidel mean: *Nes, Gadol, Hayah, Sham?*

GEOGRAPHY   574. ▶ Where is the Touro Synagogue located?

ANSWERS

CURRENT
EVENTS

568. ▶ **The destruction of Iraq's nuclear reactor deep in Iraqi territory.**

ARTS &
CULTURES

569. ▶ *The Odd Couple.* **(It was so popular it was made into a hit T.V. series.)**

PEOPLE

570. ▶ **Zev Jabotinsky.**

RELIGION

571. ▶ **One thousand years.**

HISTORY

572. ▶ **The Roman Empire.**

LANGUAGE

573. ▶ **A "great miracle happened there" (referring to the one day supply of oil that burned for eight days).**

GEOGRAPHY

574. ▶ **Newport, Rhode Island.**

CURRENT
EVENTS

575. ► How many different houses of government are there in the Israeli Knesset?

ARTS &
CULTURES

576. ► This Jewish cartoonist was so well known for his wacky and complicated inventions that his name is now used to describe any crazy device...?

PEOPLE

577. ► This philanthropic Frenchman established the wine industry in Palestine, to help the early Jewish settlers...?

RELIGION

578. ► On this holiday, traditional families decorate their homes with flowers and plants to highlight nature...?

HISTORY

579. ► Why is the Roman siege of Masada remembered to this day?

LANGUAGE

580. ► The Yiddish word connoting the swinging forward and backwards during praying is...?

GEOGRAPHY

581. ► The old Biblical expression "From Dan to Beer-Sheba" referred to...?

ANSWERS

575. ► One.

576. ► Rube Goldberg.

577. ► Baron Edmond de Rothschild.

578. ► *Shavuoth.*

579. ► The Jewish fighters all committed suicide, rather than face enslavement (and be forced into idolatry).

580. ► *"Schockl"*ing.

581. ► The entire land of Israel.

166

CURRENT
EVENTS

582. ► What are the restrictions, if any, on membership in the Knesset upon Arab citizens of Israel?

ARTS &
CULTURES

583. ► This Sephardic Jew was a founder of the Impressionist Movement and painted English and Parisian landscapes and street scenes...?

PEOPLE

584. ► This Jewish entrepreneur is the owner of one of the largest private trading corporations in the United States...?

RELIGION

585. ► He was the Hercules of the Bible...?

HISTORY

586. ► There were at least seven nations that lived in Canaan before it was conquered by Israel. Name any two of these nations...?

LANGUAGE

587. ► What is meant by the religious descriptive term *frum*?

GEOGRAPHY

588. ► Which mineral, helpful in agriculture, is found in large deposits in the Negev Desert?

ANSWERS

582. ► None.

583. ► Camille Pisarro.

584. ► Michel Fribourg (owner of The Continental Grain Company).

585. ► Samson.

586. ► (Any two of these): Jebusites; Canaanites; Perizzites; Amorites; Giorgashites; Hivites; Hittites (Exodus).

587. ► One who is completely observant of Jewish religious laws and customs.

588. ► Phosphates.

CURRENT
EVENTS   **589.** ► Israel's "Bar Lev" line refers to...?

ARTS &
CULTURES   **590.** ► This type of Judaism advocates modifications of Orthodoxy to deal with contemporary life and thought...?

PEOPLE   **591.** ► After Antiochus Epiphanes desecrated the Temple and the Jewish people resisted, who was the most memorable Jewish war hero to emerge from this conflict?

RELIGION   **592.** ► Who refrained from eating and drinking for 40 days and where did he do this?

HISTORY   **593.** ► What was decided in 1942 Germany, at the "Wannsee Conference"?

LANGUAGE   **594.** ► The name Palestine originated from...?

GEOGRAPHY   **595.** ► This is Israel's largest river...?

ANSWERS

589. ▶ Israeli fortifications on the Sinai side of the Suez Canal, built after the Six-Day War and named after General Bar Lev.

590. ▶ Reform Judaism.

591. ▶ Judah Maccabee.

592. ▶ Moses, on Mount Sinai.

593. ▶ The Nazis decided to implement the "Final Solution."

594. ▶ The Biblical reference to the land of the Philistines.

595. ▶ The Jordan River.

CURRENT
EVENTS

596. ► How many Arab states are fighting against the existence of Israel?

ARTS &
CULTURES

597. ► This Jewish songwriter is one of America's best known pop composers, with the hits: "Walk on By," "Raindrops Keep Fallin' on My Head," and more...?

PEOPLE

598. ► Marranos were secret Jews from these two countries...?

RELIGION

599. ► He was the first English Jew to join the House of Lords...?

HISTORY

600. ► This one position in the British Empire is closed to Jews...?

LANGUAGE

601. ► In which century was the exiled Jewish population of England permitted to return?

GEOGRAPHY

602. ► Eilat is located on the shore of this body of water...?

ANSWERS

CURRENT EVENTS   596. ► Twenty-one.

ARTS & CULTURES   597. ► Burt Bacharach.

PEOPLE   598. ► Spain and Portugal.

RELIGION   599. ► Nathaniel Rothschild.

HISTORY   600. ► The position of Monarch.

LANGUAGE   601. ► The 17th (1656).

GEOGRAPHY   602. ► The Red Sea.

CURRENT
EVENTS

603. ► The Israeli *Histadrut* is...?

ARTS &
CULTURES

604. ► What is the title of the well-known biography of Michelangelo, by Irving Stone?

PEOPLE

605. ► What device was Jewish scientist Edward Teller connected with?

RELIGION

606. ► Why does Judaism regard life as a ladder?

HISTORY

607. ► Where is the largest concentration of Jews ever?

LANGUAGE

608. ► The Hebrew expression *Am Israel Chai* translates to...?

GEOGRAPHY

609. ► The ancient village of Pekiin, located in what is now northern Israel, is the only city that has always had a Jewish population since Biblical times. Why is this symbolically and legally important?

ANSWERS

CURRENT
EVENTS **603.** ► A network of labor unions organized by craft, founded in 1920 by David Ben-Gurion.

ARTS &
CULTURES **604.** ► *The Agony and the Ecstasy.*

PEOPLE **605.** ► The hydrogen bomb.

RELIGION **606.** ► Because each person can achieve the highest height or sink to the lowest depth depending on his or her values, ethics and accomplishments.

HISTORY **607.** ► The New York metropolitan area.

LANGUAGE **608.** ► "The People of Israel Live."

GEOGRAPHY **609.** ► It supports the claim that Israel is the rightful land of the Jewish people since they have always maintained some presence there.

CURRENT
EVENTS   610. ▶ Why are some ultra Orthodox Jews opposed to the State of Israel and its
governing laws?

ARTS &
CULTURES   611. ▶ This famous Jewish musician is
America's most successful conductor,
composer and pianist. He also composed several famous theatrical musical scores...?

PEOPLE   612. ▶ The *Falashas*, a tribe of black Jews,
claim that they are descendants of this
tribe of Israel...?

RELIGION   613. ▶ The *Mahzor* is used on this
occasion...?

HISTORY   614. ▶ After the Ten Commandments were
expanded to become a code of life for
the Jewish people, what were they
known as?

LANGUAGE   615. ▶ Spain repealed its notorious expulsion
of Jews in this century...?

GEOGRAPHY   616. ▶ Except for Rachel, the Matriarchs and
Patriarchs are buried here...?

ANSWERS

CURRENT
EVENTS 610. ▶ Because they believe that a homeland
for the Jewish people can only be
created by the coming of the
Messiah, and that the law of a Jewish
homeland should come from the
Torah and Talmud and not be created
through Knesset votes.

ARTS &
CULTURES 611. ▶ Leonard Bernstein.

PEOPLE 612. ▶ The Levites.

RELIGION 613. ▶ It is the prayer book used on the High
Holy Days.

HISTORY 614. ▶ The Torah or The Five Books of
Moses.

LANGUAGE 615. ▶ The nineteenth.

GEOGRAPHY 616. ▶ The Cave of Machpelah.

CURRENT
EVENTS

617. ► What is one of Israel's major industries, involving the finishing of a raw product?

ARTS &
CULTURES

618. ► This game has had a preponderance of Jewish champions...?

PEOPLE

619. ► The leading Jewish scholar of his time, Rabbi Shlomo Yitzchaki, became better known by an acronym for his name...?

RELIGION

620. ► Jerusalem is the focal point of celebration for these three major well-known Holy days, in the Jewish calendar...?

HISTORY

621. ► During which half of what century did most European nations grant Jews equal rights?

LANGUAGE

622. ► The Yiddish description of food as *Fleishig* means...?

GEOGRAPHY

623. ► What two countries have the fourth and fifth largest Jewish populations in the world?

ANSWERS

CURRENT EVENTS	**617.** ► **Diamond finishing.**
ARTS & CULTURES	**618.** ► **Chess.**
PEOPLE	**619.** ► **Rashi.**
RELIGION	**620.** ► **The three Pilgrim festivals: Pesach, Succoth, Shavuoth.**
HISTORY	**621.** ► **The last half of the 19th century.**
LANGUAGE	**622.** ► **It is meat.**
GEOGRAPHY	**623.** ► **France and Britain, respectively.**

CURRENT
EVENTS

624. ► What were the two major reasons that the Israeli government tried and prosecuted Adolph Eichmann for his crimes of genocide?

ARTS &
CULTURES

625. ► This Jewish comedian and host of the old "Texaco Star Theater" show, was well known as "Mr. Television" for his success on T.V. from 1948 to 1955...?

PEOPLE

626. ► This famous Jewish financier was known as "The Diamond King" because of his vast wealth from the South African diamond mines...?

RELIGION

627. ► These two books in the Bible are named for women...?

HISTORY

628. ► What was the approximate Jewish population of Israel when the state was formed in 1948?

LANGUAGE

629. ► When a *dreidel* lands on the side that reads *nun* it means the player is entitled to...?

GEOGRAPHY

630. ► Where were the first three Zionist Congresses held?

ANSWERS

624. ► To insure that the world thoroughly understood the true horrors of the Holocaust, and to demonstrate that the Jewish state follows the principles of due process of law.

625. ► Milton Berle.

626. ► Barney Barnatto.

627. ► Ruth and Esther.

628. ► 650,000.

629. ► Nothing (or *nichts*).

630. ► in Basle, Switzerland (the first one was in 1897).

CURRENT
EVENTS
631. ► What did Israel's Rina Mor-Messinger do on July 11th, 1976, that made her a first?

ARTS &
CULTURES
632. ► This Jewish author wrote the book *The Winds of War*...?

PEOPLE
633. ► This wealthy Jewish family is best known for their movie theaters and hotels...?

RELIGION
634. ► The *Simchat Bat* refers to...?

HISTORY
635. ► What was Israel's "Operation Magic Carpet"?

LANGUAGE
636. ► The Hebrew word *Siddur* refers to this...?

GEOGRAPHY
637. ► This street in old Venice was known as a walking concourse for Jews...?

ANSWERS

631. ► She became the first entrant from Israel to win the Miss Universe title.

632. ► Herman Wouk.

633. ► The Tisch family.

634. ► "The joy of having a daughter"—it is a home celebration on the Friday evening following the birth of a girl.

635. ► The rescue of 50,000 Yemenite Jews on 430 air flights to Israel, from 1949 to 1950.

636. ► A prayer book.

637. ► The Rialto.

Trivia Judaica™   **QUESTIONS**

CURRENT
EVENTS

638. ► What was Israel's "Operation Redemption," on July 4th, 1976?

ARTS &
CULTURES

639. ► This Jewish actor starred as Zelig...?

PEOPLE

640. ► This wealthy French Jewish philanthropist generously supported the early Jewish settlements in Palestine...?

RELIGION

641. ► How long did Methuselah live?

HISTORY

642. ► What was the major argument by wealthy established Jews, against Theodore Herzl's ideas for a Jewish homeland?

LANGUAGE

643. ► A *Chassen* is Yiddish for...?

GEOGRAPHY

644. ► This pre-World War II, Canadian city had the largest Jewish population in Canada...?

ANSWERS

CURRENT EVENTS
638. ► The raid on Entebbe Airport to rescue the hostages taken prisoner by Arab prisoners.

ARTS & CULTURES
639. ► Woody Allen.

PEOPLE
640. ► Baron Edmond de Rothschild.

RELIGION
641. ► 969 years.

HISTORY
642. ► That Jews should assimilate in the countries where they lived and gain acceptance rather than aspire to move to a Jewish homeland and create suspicion and bad will against those remaining behind.

LANGUAGE
643. ► A bridegroom.

GEOGRAPHY
644. ► Montreal.

CURRENT
EVENTS

645. ► What event directly preceded the entry of Israeli troops into Lebanon, in 1982?

ARTS &
CULTURES

646. ► What is the American classification of writing in which Yiddish literature has achieved a special distinct status in the U.S.?

PEOPLE

647. ► He dedicted his entire life to the Jewish people. He formed the "Conference of Claims" against Germany and successfully negotiated reparation payments to Jews. He was the President of the World Zionist Organization for 12 years until 1968, and he co-edited the *Encylopedia Judaica*...?

RELIGION

648. ► From what man is the Messiah supposed to descend?

HISTORY

649. ► What did Miriam discover that was eventually significant to the Jewish people?

LANGUAGE

650. ► The Jewish concept of *Pikuach Nefesh* means...?

GEOGRAPHY

651. ► Where is the Stern College for Women located?

ANSWERS

CURRENT
EVENTS **645.** ▶ The attempted assassination of Israel's Ambassador to Great Britain.

ARTS &
CULTURES **646.** ▶ Poetry.

PEOPLE **647.** ▶ Nahum Goldmann.

RELIGION **648.** ▶ David.

HISTORY **649.** ▶ Moses, floating in the Nile.

LANGUAGE **650.** ▶ The guarding of life.

GEOGRAPHY **651.** ▶ New York City (it is a division of Yeshiva University).

CURRENT
EVENTS
652. ► Who was the fourth Israeli Prime Minister, serving from 1962-1968?

ARTS &
CULTURES
653. ► What controversial Jewish sports announcer was born with the name Howard Cohen?

PEOPLE
654. ► He was in the U.S. Senate for 24 yeras and lost only one election in his 32 years of public service...?

RELIGION
655. ► Who censured Joshua, saying: "Art thou jealous for my sake? Would that all the Lord's people were prophets, that the Lord would put his spirits upon them"...?

HISTORY
656. ► What was UNSCOP?

LANGUAGE
657. ► A *Kalleh* is Yiddish for...?

GEOGRAPHY
658. ► Mount Carmel is located in this major Israeli city...?

ANSWERS

CURRENT
EVENTS   652. ▶ Levi Eshkol.

ARTS &
CULTURES   653. ▶ Howard Cosell.

PEOPLE   654. ▶ Jacob Javits.

RELIGION   655. ▶ Moses. (Joshua received this rebuke
                     when he told him that others were
                     diminishing his authority by prophe-
                     sizing also.)

HISTORY   656. ▶ U.N. Special Committee on Palestine,
                     which recommended the Resolution
                     of November 29, 1947.

LANGUAGE   657. ▶ A bride.

GEOGRAPHY   658. ▶ Haifa.

CURRENT
EVENTS
659. ► The approximate 1984 Jewish population of Israel is...?

ARTS &
CULTURES
660. ► He was the best known of Cantors referred to as "The Jewish Caruso"...?

PEOPLE
661. ► He was the first President of Israel...?

RELIGION
662. ► How did the name "Passover" originate?

HISTORY
663. ► This king of the divided Kingdom of Israel, introduced the pagan worship of the idol Ba'al...?

LANGUAGE
664. ► The complete Hebrew expression for "Peace be with you" is...?

GEOGRAPHY
665. ► This street in Israel is named Ben Maimon Street, after a famous 11th century Jewish philosopher. He is more commonly known as...?

ANSWERS

659. ▶ **Three million.**

660. ▶ **Joseph Rosenblatt.**

661. ▶ **Chaim Weitzman.**

662. ▶ **Moses promised that G-d would "pass over" the houses of the Jews when the Egyptian firstborn were dying.**

663. ▶ **King Ahab.**

664. ▶ *Shalom Aleichem.*

665. ▶ **Moses Maimonides or Rambam-Rabenu or Moshe ben Maimon.**

CURRENT
EVENTS
666. ► Three major security and political issues still confronting Israel since the 1967 Six-Day War are...?

ARTS &
CULTURES
667. ► What famous French Jewish painter was born with the name Moshe Segal?

PEOPLE
668. ► This distinguished lawyer and Harvard Law School professor defended *Deep Throat*'s Harry Reems, and the Russian dissident Anatoly Sharansky...?

RELIGION
669. ► There are several Biblical occurrences and references that involve the number 10. Two of these are...?

HISTORY
670. ► Throughout history, Christians have accused Jews of the "ritual murder" of Christians. What were their specific allegations?

LANGUAGE
671. ► In English, *Chanukah* means...?

GEOGRAPHY
672. ► This Port is Israel's gateway to the East...?

ANSWERS

CURRENT EVENTS 666. ► Secure and internationally recognized borders; Arab recognition of Israel; and a lasting peace treaty.

ARTS & CULTURES 667. ► Marc Chagall.

PEOPLE 668. ► Allan Dershowitz.

RELIGION 669. ► Any two of these: the ten plagues (Exodus); The ten brothers of Joseph who went to Egypt to buy grain (Genesis); the ten tribes of Israel; the Ten Commandments (Exodus).

HISTORY 670. ► Usually, that Jews use the blood of Christian children to make matzos for Passover.

LANGUAGE 671. ► "Dedication".

GEOGRAPHY 672. ► Eilat.

CURRENT EVENTS

673. ► The approximate 1984 Jewish population of Russia is...?

ARTS & CULTURES

674. ► This author wrote *The Rich Jew of Malta*...?

PEOPLE

675. ► Toscanini's daughter married this famous Jewish pianist...?

RELIGION

676. ► How did the ancient Jews capture the town of Jericho?

HISTORY

677. ► Why did large numbers of Jews come to Poland and Lithuania during the Middle Ages?

LANGUAGE

678. ► The English translation of the word *pogrom* is...?

GEOGRAPHY

679. ► The Bible often refers to either Jerusalem or this other place that is also considered to be a synonym for Jerusalem...?

ANSWERS

673. ► 2.75 million.

674. ► Christopher Marlowe.

675. ► Vladimir Horowitz.

676. ► Joshua had the walls destroyed by horn blowing and instructing the Israelites to circle the walls 7 times.

677. ► To escape persecution.

678. ► Riot.

679. ► "Zion."

CURRENT
EVENTS

680. ► How frequently are Israeli elections held and are there are any exceptions?

ARTS &
CULTURES

681. ► This Jewish actress was born as Betty Jean Perske and was nicknamed "Bogey's Baby"...?

PEOPLE

682. ► He was the most anti-Semitic of composers...?

RELIGION

683. ► Which historical events do *Succoth* and *Shavuoth* serve to commemorate?

HISTORY

684. ► What was the main reason that Karl Marx viewed Judaism with disdain?

LANGUAGE

685. ► When a *dreidel* lands on the side that reads *gimmel* it means...?

GEOGRAPHY

686. ► Where was the "Good Fence" located?

ANSWERS

680. ▶ **They are supposed to take place every four years, but Parliament can be dissolved at any time, and new elections called.**

681. ▶ **Lauren Bacall.**

682. ▶ **Richard Wagner.**

683. ▶ ***Succoth*: The desert journey of the Jews on their way to the Promised Land. *Shavuoth*: The giving of the Torah.**

684. ▶ **He thought it was too involved with capitalism.**

685. ▶ **Take all.**

686. ▶ **Between Israel and Lebanon (it was a border crossing).**

CURRENT
EVENTS
    687. ▶ Name the three Israeli prime ministers starting, in chronological order, after Levi Eshkol...?

ARTS &
CULTURES
    688. ▶ Who is the most famous Jewish country music star?

PEOPLE
    689. ▶ This respected Jewish clan, originally of German background, started their distinguished careers in the Woodrow Wilson administration, served in Roosevelt's cabinet, and served as attorney general of New York State...?

RELIGION
    690. ▶ What is the significance of the candelabras that all synagogues are decorated with?

HISTORY
    691. ▶ The land of Israel was repeatedly sought by at least 8 ancient empires for this major reason?

LANGUAGE
    692. ▶ What is the literal meaning of the term "rabbi"?

GEOGRAPHY
    693. ▶ Israel's commemoration of: the Holocaust, Jewish resistance and heroism can be seen at this place...?

ANSWERS

687. ► Golda Meir, Yitzack Rabin, Menachem Begin.

688. ► "Kinky Friedman and The Texas Jewboys".

689. ► The Morganthaus.

690. ► They connote light and life itself. (They originally were found in the Holy Temple.)

691. ► It was the connecting bridge between three continents, serving as a crossroad for the ancient world.

692. ► "My master."

693. ► Yad Vashem Museum, on Mt. Herzlia, Jerusalem.

CURRENT
EVENTS

694. ► What is the name of the Israeli-manufactured tank?

ARTS &
CULTURES

695. ► This famous Jewish songwriter wrote "Easter Parade" and "White Christmas"...?

PEOPLE

696. ► This Jewish clothing manufacturer immigrated to the U.S. from Bavaria, in the 19th century, and became a clothing superstar with his new product...?

RELIGION

697. ► The religious concept of monotheism stands for...?

HISTORY

698. ► This brutal Russian group was known for its violent actions against Jews...?

LANGUAGE

699. ► The Hebrew word for "good dead" is...?

GEOGRAPHY

700. ► This large emblem is located next to the entrance of Israel's Knesset building and was a gift from the British government...?

ANSWERS

694. ▶ "Merkava" or the Chariot Tank.

695. ▶ Irving Berlin.

696. ▶ Levi Strauss (the blue jean).

697. ▶ One god. (This concept began in Judaism and has expanded to all major religions.)

698. ▶ The "Cossacks."

699. ▶ *Mitzvah.*

700. ▶ A gigantic Menorah.

CURRENT
EVENTS
701. ► Why are native-born Israelis called Sabras?

ARTS &
CULTURES
702. ► This Jewish band leader was known as "The King of Swing"...?

PEOPLE
703. ► Who on the America First committee said in 1941, that "Jews are pushing America towards war with Germany"?

RELIGION
704. ► The "Sabbath of Sabbaths" refers to this day...?

HISTORY
705. ► From 1948 to 1984 approximately how many Jews have made *Aliyah* to Israel?

LANGUAGE
706. ► What is the "Magen David Adom"?

GEOGRAPHY
707. ► The Jews of Southern Arabia are known in modern times as the Jews of this country...?

ANSWERS

701. ▶ A "Sabra" is a cactus fruit and, like this fruit, Isaelis are said to be tough on the suface and soft and sweet on the inside.

702. ▶ Benny Goodman.

703. ▶ Colonel Charles Lindbergh.

704. ▶ *Yom Kippur*.

705. ▶ Over 2.5 million.

706. ▶ The Israeli "Red Cross".

707. ▶ Yemen.

CURRENT EVENTS   **708.** ► What is the most common serious genetic disease to affect Jews?

ARTS & CULTURES   **709.** ► This Jewish Rumanian born artist created the well-known cover of the *New Yorker,* which became a popular poster depicting a view of America from New York City...?

PEOPLE   **710.** ► This Jewish publisher began as an immigrant from Hungary and eventually controlled *The New York World* and *The St. Louis Post-Dispatch.* He also financed the Columbia University School of Journalism...?

RELIGION   **711.** ► What does the *Chanukah* holiday commemorate?

HISTORY   **712.** ► What empire controlled Palestine, prior to World War I?

LANGUAGE   **713.** ► The popularized Hebrew word for impudence is...?

GEOGRAPHY   **714.** ► This European city was nicknamed "The Jerusalem of Lithuania"...?

ANSWERS

CURRENT
EVENTS
708. ► Tay-Sachs Disease.

ARTS &
CULTURES
709. ► Steinberg.

PEOPLE
710. ► Joseph Pulitzer.

RELIGION
711. ► The victory of the Maccabees over the Syrians, and the liberation of the Temple in Jerusalem.

HISTORY
712. ► The Ottoman Turkish Empire.

LANGUAGE
713. ► *Chutzpah.*

GEOGRAPHY
714. ► Vilna.

CURRENT
EVENTS
715. ► Israel's "Open Bridges" policy refers to...?

ARTS &
CULTURES
716. ► This Jewish author wrote *World of Our Fathers* and is the editor of *Dissent* magazine...?

PEOPLE
717. ► He was the first Jewish settler in Canada...?

RELIGION
718. ► What is the general difference between Jewish holidays and Jewish festivals?

HISTORY
719. ► What was the main inspiration for the Jewish flag's design?

LANGUAGE
720. ► *Ulpan* is what type of program?

GEOGRAPHY
721. ► The ancient city of Megiddo has become famous throughout history because of the many battles fought there. What does it symbolize in literature?

ANSWERS

CURRENT EVENTS
715. ► Keeping the Jordan River bridges open so that West Bank Arabs can maintain economic and cultural ties with Jordan.

ARTS & CULTURES
716. ► Irving Howe.

PEOPLE
717. ► Aaron Hart.

RELIGION
718. ► Holidays are religious celebrations while festivals are historical and ethnic celebrations.

HISTORY
719. ► The Jewish prayer shawl.

LANGUAGE
720. ► A study and living program for new students of Hebrew.

GEOGRAPHY
721. ► The final battle between civilization's opposite ideologies.

CURRENT
EVENTS
   722. ► What Israeli political party was the key to the formation of Prime Minister Begin's second Government of July, 1981?

ARTS &
CULTURES
   723. ► In 1976, this Jewish writer was the first American to win the Nobel Prize for Literature since Steinbeck in 1962. He generally writes about Jews and their love for America...?

PEOPLE
   724. ► Both John F. Kennedy and Albert Einstein are memorialized in the same manner in Israel...?

RELIGION
   725. ► This young Jewish lawyer gained fame as committee counsel at the McCarthy Hearings of the early 1950's, and has recently been frequently in the news because of his well known clientele...?

HISTORY
   726. ► At the beginning of World War I, what percentage of world Jewry lived in countries where they did not enjoy equal rights?

LANGUAGE
   727. ► Jews were the creators of this type of American retail business...?

GEOGRAPHY
   728. ► What are the Qumran Caves most famous for?

ANSWERS

722. ▶ The "Mafdal" or National Religious
Party.

723. ▶ Saul Bellow.

724. ▶ Forests were planted in their memory
by the Jewish National Fund.

725. ▶ Roy Cohn.

726. ▶ Fifty percent.

727. ▶ The department store.

728. ▶ The Dead Sea Scrolls were recovered
there.

CURRENT
EVENTS

729. ► The Jewish Board of Deputies represents the Jewish population of this country...?

ARTS &
CULTURES

730. ► Jan Peerce is a specialized Jewish singer in this area...?

PEOPLE

731. ► She was an outspoken liberal Jewish U.S. Congresswoman from New York known for her wide-brimmed hats...?

RELIGION

732. ► These Biblical figures, Amram, Jesse, Elkana and Terah, are the fathers of some very well known heroes. Name their sons...?

HISTORY

733. ► What was the Jewish National Fund's original and main purpose?

LANGUAGE

734. ► The traditional hymn "Maoz Tzur", in English means...?

GEOGRAPHY

735. ► In what part of New York City was the old time radio and T.V. show "The Goldbergs" situated?

ANSWERS

729. ▶ England.

730. ▶ An opera tenor.

731. ▶ Bella Abzug.

732. ▶ Moses and Amram (Exodus); David
and Jesse (Ruth); Samuel and Elkana
(Samuel); Abraham and Terah
(Genesis).

733. ▶ To buy land in Palestine and lease it to
Jewish farmers.

734. ▶ "Rock of Ages."

735. ▶ The Bronx.

CURRENT
EVENTS

736. ▶ On June 7, 1981, Israel was responsible for a successful "first-ever" in the area of disarmament. What did they do?

ARTS &
CULTURES

737. ▶ Philip Glass is Jewish and an avant-garde success in this musical field...?

PEOPLE

738. ▶ Who was the second Israeli Prime Minister, serving from 1954-1955?

RELIGION

739. ▶ What was the first battle in which Joshua led the Jews?

HISTORY

740. ▶ What military event resulted in the deaths of 50 to 90 percent of the Jewish population of Judea and the exile of Jews from their land...?

LANGUAGE

741. ▶ The Hebrew word for "pioneer" is...?

GEOGRAPHY

742. ▶ When did Jerusalem first become the capital of Israel?

ANSWERS

736. ▶ They forcibly disarmed Iraq from its nuclear weapons program with a pre-emptive strike on their nuclear reactor.

737. ▶ Composing (he wrote "Einstein on the Beach").

738. ▶ Moshe Sharett.

739. ▶ Jericho.

740. ▶ The Bar Kochba Revolt (in 135 B.C.E.)

741. ▶ *Chalutz.*

742. ▶ 1948.

743. ► What respected world figure was involved in this controversial 1982 meeting with an international terrorist, causing the Israeli government to express their "profound disappointment". They claimed that it would be "recorded in the national memory of the State of Israel and the Jewish people"...?

ARTS &
CULTURES 744. ► Which old-time Jewish movie mogul was born with the name Samuel Goldfish?

PEOPLE 745. ► This famous English Jewish statesman was known as the Earl of Beaconfield in the mid-1800s...?

RELIGION 746. ► What was the original language of the Bible?

HISTORY 747. ► What is "Young Judea"?

LANGUAGE 748. ► Where did the word "manna" come from?

GEOGRAPHY 749. ► In what geographic part of Israel is the Galilee located?

ANSWERS

743. ► Pope John Paul II and Yasir Arafat.

744. ► Samuel Goldwyn.

745. ► Benjamin Disraeli.

746. ► Hebrew.

747. ► The oldest and largest youth movement in the U.S.

748. ► It evolved when the ancient Israelites first saw it and they exlaimed "Ma nu?" – meaning, "What is it?"

749. ► The most northern section.

CURRENT
EVENTS

750. ► How many members are there in the Israeli Knesset?

ARTS &
CULTURES

751. ► Jewish artist Chaim Gross is known as a great...?

PEOPLE

752. ► This American Jewish family owns the largest communications conglomerate in the world...?

RELIGION

753. ► How many times was the Temple built, and by whom was it built each time?

HISTORY

754. ► Against whom was Moshe Dayan fighting when he lost his left eye?

LANGUAGE

755. ► What is the literal meaning and then the slang meaning of *Nebish*?

GEOGRAPHY

756. ► Name three of the five major land areas captured and occupied by Israel in the 1967 Six-Day War...?

ANSWERS

CURRENT
EVENTS **750.** ► **120.**

ARTS &
CULTURES **751.** ► **Sculptor.**

PEOPLE **752.** ► **The Newhouse family.**

RELIGION **753.** ► **Three times: by Solomon, by Zeru-babel and by Herod.**

HISTORY **754.** ► **He was fighting with the Israeli "Palmach," or "Strike Forces", against Vichy-French troops in Syria (in 1941).**

LANGUAGE **755.** ► **Literally, it means "alas"; in slang, it means a "chronic loser".**

GEOGRAPHY **756.** ► **(Any three of these): The West Bank, the Sinai Peninsula, East Jerusalem, the Golan Heights, and the Gaza Strip.**

CURRENT
EVENTS   757. ► What government position did Ezer Weizman hold in the 1977 to 1979 Israeli leadership?

ARTS &
CULTURES   758. ► This famous Jewish composer wrote the song "God Bless America"...?

PEOPLE   759. ► She established the "Youth Aliyah" movement, approximately 40 years ago...?

RELIGION   760. ► What does *Simchat Torah* celebrate?

HISTORY   761. ► According to the Bible, these two Israelites defeated an entire Philistine army...?

LANGUAGE   762. ► What does *Dybbuk* refer to?

GEOGRAPHY   763. ► Moses Maimonides was born here...?

ANSWERS

CURRENT EVENTS **757.** ► Defense Minister.

ARTS & CULTURES **758.** ► Irving Berlin.

PEOPLE **759.** ► Henrietta Szold, to help the orphans of the Holocaust.

RELIGION **760.** ► The yearly completion of weekly Torah readings.

HISTORY **761.** ► Jonathan and his armor-bearer. (The enemy thought that the reason they were so bold to approach them alone was because there must have been an army behind them.)

LANGUAGE **762.** ► One who is possessed.

GEOGRAPHY **763.** ► Spain.

CURRENT
EVENTS   **764.** ► Which recent U.S. Vice President warned against Zionist activities in the U.S.?

ARTS &
CULTURES   **765.** ► This convert to Judaism began his career in entertainment as "Silent Sam, The Dancing Midget"...?

PEOPLE   **766.** ► This wealthy Jewish family is best known for their Canadian liquor fortune...?

RELIGION   **767.** ► What do the three pieces of matza used at the Seder represent?

HISTORY   **768.** ► On this particular night three tragedies occured to the Jewish people: The First and the Second Temple of Jerusalem were destroyed, and the Jews of Spain were expelled...?

LANGUAGE   **769.** ► The *Negev* Desert literally translates into...?

GEOGRAPHY   **770.** ► When Joshua was successful in his battle for Canaan, the main victory was at this memorable city...?

ANSWERS

764. ► Spiro Agnew.

765. ► Sammy Davis, Jr.

766. ► The Bronfman family.

767. ► The three ancient categories of Jews:
Levites, Kohens and Israelites.

768. ► The night of "Tisha B'av" or the ninth
day of the Hebrew month Av.

769. ► The "Southern Desert".

770. ► Jericho.

CURRENT
EVENTS

771. ► The replacement Defense Minister of Israel during the Lebanon War was...?

ARTS &
CULTURES

772. ► This Jewish actor starred in *Freebie and the Bean, Thief, Funny Lady,* and *Chapter Two*...?

PEOPLE

773. ► He was the only Jewish chairman ever on the Board of the DuPont Corporation...?

RELIGION

774. ► The "Nine Days of Sadness" refer to...?

HISTORY

775. ► Ironically, what was the American Council for Judaism, formed in 1943, most famous for?

LANGUAGE

776. ► The Hebrew word *shammos* refers to this type of employee...?

GEOGRAPHY

777. ► This Jewish community excommunicated Baruch Spinoza...?

ANSWERS

CURRENT
EVENTS 771. ► Moshe Arens.

ARTS &
CULTURES 772. ► James Caan.

PEOPLE 773. ► Irving Shapiro.

RELIGION 774. ► The nine days before Tisha B'Av when all joyous activities are forbidden.

HISTORY 775. ► Fighting Zionism. (They were more afraid of Zionism than anti-semitism.)

LANGUAGE 776. ► A servant.

GEOGRAPHY 777. ► The Jews of Amsterdam, Holland.

CURRENT
EVENTS

778. ► What terrorist organization carried out the Lod Airport massacre on May 30th, 1972?

ARTS &
CULTURES

779. ► The book written about the greatest Jewish families in New York was called...?

PEOPLE

780. ► This German Jewish bacteriologist created a test to detect syphilis that bears his name...?

RELIGION

781. ► He did the most to organize and establish America's Orthodox movement...?

HISTORY

782. ► This Dutch company, because of its partial Jewish control, forced Peter Stuyvesant to admit Jews to New Amsterdam, against his will...?

LANGUAGE

783. ► What is the common English translated root for the words *Kiddush* and *Kaddish*?

GEOGRAPHY

784. ► Sholem Aleichem was born where?

ANSWERS

778. ► The Japanese Red Army.

779. ► *Our Crowd* (written by a gentile, Stephen Birmingham).

780. ► August von Wasserman.

781. ► Sabato Morais.

782. ► The Dutch West Indies Company.

783. ► They both stem from the word "holy".

784. ► Russia.

CURRENT
EVENTS

785. ► What Jewish groups share in the distribution of United Jewish Appeal revenues?

ARTS &
CULTURES

786. ► What two crew members of the *Starship Enterprise*, from the T.V. show *Star Trek*, are Jewish?

PEOPLE

787. ► Josephine Sarah "Sadie" Marcus was a "strictly raised girl...from a prosperous German-Jewish family" who gained fame and adventure as the wife of one of the Old West's most colorful characters. Who was he?

RELIGION

788. ► How many times must one symbolically drink wine during the Seder service?

HISTORY

789. ► What event marked the beginning of basic legal rights for the Jews of France?

LANGUAGE

790. ► What are the two explicit Jewish languages?

GEOGRAPHY

791. ► What is *Mea Shearim*?

ANSWERS

785. ► The Jewish Agency, the Joint, and local communities.

786. ► William Shatner (Captain Kirk) and Leonard Nimoy (Mr. Spock).

787. ► Wyatt Earp, the gunfighter.

788. ► Four (to symbolize and commemorate the four redemption expressions the Bible uses to describe the exodus).

789. ► The French Revolution, in 1789.

790. ► Yiddish and Ladino.

791. ► The ultra-Orthodox quarter of Jerusalem.

CURRENT
EVENTS

792. ► What is the Reagan administration's stated policy on new Israeli settlements on the West Bank, and on existing settlements in Judea and Samaria?

ARTS &
CULTURES

793. ► This Jewish comedian popularized the line: "Bisexuality doubles your chances for a date on Saturday nights"...?

PEOPLE

794. ► Pope Anacletus the Second was nicknamed...?

RELIGION

795. ► The two grand Jewish Holy Days are...?

HISTORY

796. ► What was the approximate Jewish population of the U.S. during the Revolutionary War?

LANGUAGE

797. ► The Yiddish word *babushka* means...?

GEOGRAPHY

798. ► This East European country had a popular saying among its anti-Semitic populace: "Kill the Jews and save _____". What country needed saving that way?

227

ANSWERS

792. ► They are opposed to new settlements but Jews living in existing settlements have the "right" to remain.

ARTS &
CULTURES
793. ► Woody Allen.

PEOPLE
794. ► "The Jewish Pope", because he was of Jewish heritage.

RELIGION
795. ► The Day of Atonement ("Yom Kippur") and the New Year ("Rosh Hashanah").

HISTORY
796. ► 2,500.

LANGUAGE
797. ► A kerchief for the head.

GEOGRAPHY
798. ► Russia.

CURRENT
EVENTS
799. ► In 1982, the Anti-Defamation League of B'nai B'rith made a study on the three major T.V. networks and the handling of the coverage of the War in Lebanon. The results indicated that the three all...?

ARTS &
CULTURES
800. ► This old-time Jewish comedian made famous the line "Take my wife... please"...?

PEOPLE
801. ► This famous Rabbi of almost 2,000 years ago made the "Shema" prayer famous when he repeated it while being tortured to death for refusing to stop reading the Torah...?

RELIGION
802. ► What is another English name for Yom Kippur?

HISTORY
803. ► What form of money did Abraham use to purchase the "Cave of Machpelah"?

LANGUAGE
804. ► The Yiddish expression *Baitz* refers to this nationality...?

GEOGRAPHY
805. ► Where, according to tradition, is the burial place of Queen Esther?

ANSWERS

799. ▶ "Unwittingly or unconsciously con-
tributed to some distortions and lack
of objective perspective in their coverage..."

800. ▶ Henny Youngman.

801. ▶ Rabbi Akiba.

802. ▶ The "Day of Judgment" or the "Day of
Memorial" or the "Day of Atonement".

803. ▶ Shekels (he paid 400 shekels of
silver).

804. ▶ The Irish.

805. ▶ The village of Bar'am, in northern
Israel.

CURRENT
EVENTS
806. ▶ What allegations about Nazi war criminal Klaus Barbie were being investigated by the U.S. Justice Department, in March of 1983?

ARTS &
CULTURES
807. ▶ This outrageous Jewish comedian frequently asked: "Who's buried in Grant's tomb?"...?

PEOPLE
808. ▶ What infamous company did Benjamin Siegel and Meyer Lansky found?

RELIGION
809. ▶ Moses was descended from this Tribe...?

HISTORY
810. ▶ The chief occupation in early Palestine was...?

LANGUAGE
811. ▶ The Yiddish expression *Farmisht* refers to this state of mind...?

GEOGRAPHY
812. ▶ When settlers first came to the Arava Plains area of the Negev, what was the first thing they had to do to make the soil fertile?

ANSWERS

806. ► That he worked for U.S. government agencies after World War II, and was assisted by them in his escape from Europe.

807. ► Groucho Marx (in his T.V. quiz program, *You Bet Your Life*).

808. ► Murder Incorporated.

809. ► The Levites.

810. ► Farming.

811. ► Mixed up.

812. ► They had to wash the salt out of the soil.

CURRENT
EVENTS

813. ► What personal action did Andrew Young take following criticism of his 1977 meeting with P.L.O. observers at the U.N.?

ARTS &
CULTURES

814. ► Jewish musician Andre Kostelanatz is known as a great...?

PEOPLE

815. ► Which part of horse racing's Triple Crown is named for a Jewish financier?

RELIGION

816. ► He was the last Judge, the first Prophet and he founded the ancient monarchy ...?

HISTORY

817. ► From which Tribe are most of the modern day Jews descended?

LANGUAGE

818. ► The holiday *Simchat Torah* literally means...?

GEOGRAPHY

819. ► Where is the oldest European Synagogue that is still in use?

ANSWERS

813. ► He resigned.

814. ► Conductor and composer.

815. ► The Belmont Stakes (named after August Belmont).

816. ► Samuel.

817. ► Judah.

818. ► Rejoicing of the Torah. (This is a day of happiness and total rejoicing.)

819. ► In Prague (the Old-New Synagogue, built in the 1400's).

CURRENT
EVENTS

820. ► This special athletic event occurs in Israel once every four years...?

ARTS &
CULTURES

821. ► This Biblical figure was played by Burt Lancaster in a 1975 T.V. mini-series...?

PEOPLE

822. ► This distinguished Israeli Premier said: "We do not rejoice in victories, we rejoice when strawberries bloom in Israel"...?

RELIGION

823. ► When is the proper time for Sabbath candles to be lit?

HISTORY

824. ► What experience caused Theodore Herzl to become an ardent Zionist?

LANGUAGE

825. ► *Bar Mitzvah* literally translates into...?

GEOGRAPHY

826. ► In olden times, this country has persecuted Christians, yet has been friendly to Jews...?

ANSWERS

820. ► **The Maccabiah Games.**

821. ► **Moses.**

822. ► **Golda Meir.**

823. ► **Just before sunset (Jewish religious calendars list exact times in case of cloudy days in which there are no sunsets).**

824. ► **He witnessed mobs of Frenchmen chanting "Death to the Jews" during the Dreyfus trial.**

825. ► **Son of the Commandment.**

826. ► **Turkey.**

Trivia Judaica™   **QUESTIONS**

CURRENT EVENTS

827. ► What significant event happened during this Egyptian military parade on October 6, 1981?

ARTS & CULTURES

828. ► A Jewish philanthropist donated this distinctive New York Museum, famous for its architecture...?

PEOPLE

829. ► These two Jewish 1960's radicals founded the Youth International Party and advocated total anarchy and distrust of anyone over the age of thirty...?

RELIGION

830. ► In ancient Israel, what was the role of the *Kohanim* in Jewish life?

HISTORY

831. ► This British General entered Jerusalem on foot to symbolize his reverence for its history, after he beat the Ottoman-Turks for control.

LANGUAGE

832. ► The *Haskalah* was ...?

GEOGRAPHY

833. ► Purim is the only major Jewish holiday whose story did not take place in the Holy Land. Where did it take place?

237

ANSWERS

CURRENT
EVENTS 827. ► President Sadat was assassinated.

ARTS &
CULTURES 828. ► The Guggenheim.

PEOPLE 829. ► Abbie Hoffman and Jerry Rubin.

RELIGION 830. ► They were the priests of the Jewish Tribes (descendants of Aaron).

HISTORY 831. ► General Allenby.

LANGUAGE 832. ► The term describing the Jewish "Enlightenment" or the enhancement of modern interests and western ideas, among the Jews of of Poland and Russia.

GEOGRAPHY 833. ► Persia.

CURRENT
EVENTS
834. ► What were the two major economic problems facing Israel in 1984?

ARTS &
CULTURES
835. ► What Jewish tough-guy actor was born with the name Charles Buchinsky?

PEOPLE
836. ► In the Bible, Zechariah described a scene which has been transposed on an emblem and is used as a modern day symbol: "I have seen and beheld a candlestick all of gold...and its seven branches...and two olive trees by it..." What does this symbol now represent?

RELIGION
837. ► During the Purim service, why are the names of Haman's ten sons all combined together in one long name?

HISTORY
838. ► The first Jews in America arrived in what century?

LANGUAGE
839. ► The Hebrew status of *Agunah* refers to a woman in what circumstance...?

GEOGRAPHY
840. ► What is the historic significance of Modiin?

ANSWERS

834. ► The serious decline in foreign currency reserves, and an annual inflation rate over 400%.

835. ► Charles Bronson.

836. ► The State of Israel.

837. ► To symbolize the fact that they were all hanged together for their parts in the conspiracy to massacre the Jews.

838. ► The 17th.

839. ► A woman who is not allowed to remarry because her husband has abandoned her, or if there is no proof of his death.

840. ► It was the birthplace of the Maccabees.

CURRENT
EVENTS

841. ► In August of 1982, what transpired between the Sandinista government of Nicaragua and their 50-member Jewish community?

ARTS &
CULTURES

842. ► This Jewish author wrote the best seller *The Joys of Yiddish*...?

PEOPLE

843. ► Who was Sennacherib?

RELIGION

844. ► What are the *Mitzvot*?

HISTORY

845. ► What major action, if any, did the Vatican take to discourage the genocide inflicted on the Jews during the Holocaust?

LANGUAGE

846. ► What type of food is *Mandelbroit*?

GEOGRAPHY

847. ► To what town in Canaan did the High Priest Eleazar bring the Ten Commandments for safekeeping?

ANSWERS

841. ► The Sandinista government forced the Jewish community into exile, confiscated all Jewish properties and took over Managua's Synagogue.

842. ► Leo Rosten.

843. ► The King of Assyria.

844. ► The religious duties of a Jew.

845. ► There was no intervention.

846. ► A pastry.

847. ► "Shiloh" (which then became the main religious center for the Jews).

CURRENT
EVENTS

848. ► What presidential candidate referred to potential Jewish voters as "Hymies" creating a furor in the Jewish community?

ARTS &
CULTURES

849. ► What was the constant theme dominating Jehudah Halevi's poetry?

PEOPLE

850. ► This early Zionist said, "If you will it, it is no fable"...?

RELIGION

851. ► How many days are there in *Shiva*?

HISTORY

852. ► For how many years did the Ottoman Turks rule Jerusalem and Palestine?

LANGUAGE

853. ► What does the name *Joshua* mean?

GEOGRAPHY

854. ► The *Darom* refers to this part of Israel...?

ANSWERS

CURRENT
EVENTS   **848. ▶ The Reverend Jesse Jackson.**

ARTS &
CULTURES   **849. ▶ Love of Jerusalem (or Zion).**

PEOPLE   **850. ▶ Theodore Hertzl.**

RELIGION   **851. ▶ Seven days.**

HISTORY   **852. ▶ Four hundred years.**

LANGUAGE   **853. ▶ "G-d will save."**

GEOGRAPHY   **854. ▶ The south.**

CURRENT
EVENTS
   855. ► This Jewish writer described his year of imprisonment without trial in the book, *Prisoner Without a Name, Cell Without a Number*. . .?

ARTS &
CULTURES
   856. ► One of this Jewish folk singer's greatest hits was "This Land is Your Land". . .?

PEOPLE
   857. ► This Jewish physicist directed the Atomic Energy Research Project during World War II. . .?

RELIGION
   858. ► It is forbidden to eat meat the first nine days of this Hebrew month. . .?

HISTORY
   859. ► The Wailing Wall was built higher with smaller stones on top of the large blocks of the Temple base. What ancient group was responsible for this construction?

LANGUAGE
   860. ► The Jewish scholar Judah Ha-Nasi organized this religious book. . .?

GEOGRAPHY
   861. ► What were the three worst European countries for Jews to live in immediately after World War I?

ANSWERS

855. ► Jacobo Timerman (of Argentina).

856. ► Woody Guthrie.

857. ► Robert Oppenheimer.

858. ► Av (to symbolize grief over the destruction of the Temple).

859. ► The Turks.

860. ► The *Mishna*.

861. ► Russia, Poland and Roumania.

CURRENT
EVENTS

862. ► What was unique about the proposed coalition agreement that was to resolve the stalemate confronting the Israeli government, after the inconclusive July, 1984 elections?

ARTS &
CULTURES

863. ► This tough-guy actor was originally named Emanuel Goldenberg...?

PEOPLE

864. ► Who was Nebuchadnezzar?

RELIGION

865. ► Why are there no images, statues or portraits found in Synagogues?

HISTORY

866. ► How many Tribes of Israel received the land East of the Jordan, and how many received the land on the West?

LANGUAGE

867. ► A legal hearing which is held in accordance with the rules of *Halachah* is called...?

GEOGRAPHY

868. ► The city of Netanya was named after this American Ambassador to Turkey who aided the new settlement, and the colonies of Palestine...?

ANSWERS

CURRENT
EVENTS 862. ► The heads of the two leading political parties proposed that they would take turns as "Alternate Prime Ministers".

ARTS &
CULTURES 863. ► Edward G. Robinson.

PEOPLE 864. ► The King of Babylonia.

RELIGION 865. ► For fear that their presence might encourage idolatry, which would be a violation of the Ten Commandments.

HISTORY 866. ► Two and a half tribes received the Eastern land; nine and a half tribes received the Western land.

LANGUAGE 867. ► *Din Torah.*

GEOGRAPHY 868. ► Nathan Straus.

CURRENT
EVENTS

869. ► Whose names are found in Israel's "Golden Book" in Jerusalem?

ARTS &
CULTURES

870. ► This Jewish comedian wrote and directed the movie called *The Producers*...?

PEOPLE

871. ► Laszlo Loewenstein changed his name and eventually became a famous movie star. In *Casablanca*, he played opposite Humphrey Bogart and his real first name, Laszlo, was used. What did he change his name to?

RELIGION

872. ► What is the difference between the ancient traditional Menorah and the Chanukah Menorah?

HISTORY

873. ► When were the Jews banned from dwelling in Jerusalem, while still being allowed to visit?

LANGUAGE

874. ► What must one do to become an *Oleh*?

GEOGRAPHY

875. ► *Shechem Gate, Sha-ar Shechem,* or *Nablus Gate* are names for this same Gate in the Old City of Jerusalem. It is also referred to by the same name as an Arab capital...?

ANSWERS

CURRENT
EVENTS 869. ► The names of the generous con-
tributors to the Jewish national fund.

ARTS &
CULTURES 870. ► Mel Brooks.

PEOPLE 871. ► Peter Lorre.

RELIGION 872. ► The ancient menorah had seven
branches; the *Chanukah* menorah has
eight.

HISTORY 873. ► During the "Crusaders' Kingdom of
Jerusalem," in the tenth century. (This
ban lasted 87 years.)

LANGUAGE 874. ► Emigrate to Israel.

GEOGRAPHY 875. ► Damascus Gate.

CURRENT
EVENTS

876. ► This famous Jewish public servant negotiated for the U.S. in the first SALT talks with the Russians...?

ARTS &
CULTURES

877. ► The ancient Hebrews learned mechanical subjects from this group...?

PEOPLE

878. ► This Jewish born philosopher stated that "Religion is the opiate of the masses"...?

RELIGION

879. ► This Biblical story relates the most blatant example of idol worshipping...?

HISTORY

880. ► The crimes committed in the Nazi concentration camp Theresienstadt were so terrible that a special liturgy for the victims was added by the Conservative movement into the Conservative Prayer Book. What were these crimes?

LANGUAGE

881. ► What are the three major names that the Bible uses to refer to Jews?

GEOGRAPHY

882. ► Jerusalem was given this special status according to the 1947 U.N. Partition Resolution...?

ANSWERS

876. ► **Henry Kissinger.**

877. ► **The Phoenicians.**

878. ► **Karl Marx.**

879. ► **The story of the "Golden Calf" (made
in the desert by the Hebrews, in the
absence of Moses who was on Mt.
Sinai) (Exodus).**

880. ► **The murder of 150,000 Jewish
children.**

881. ► **Jews, Israelites and Hebrews.**

882. ► **The status of an International City.**

CURRENT
EVENTS
883. ► Which U.S. General and Chairman of the U.S. Joint Chiefs of Staff, stated that Israel was a "military burden" to the U.S., in a widely publicized 1976 interview with the *Chicago Sun Times*?

ARTS &
CULTURES
884. ► During the Middle Ages, Jews enjoyed the greatest prosperity and expanded their culture most under the rule of this group...?

PEOPLE
885. ► This U.S. chess champion converted from Judaism to become Protestant...?

RELIGION
886. ► The Bible expresses what the optimal attitude toward one's neighbor should be. Quote this Biblical sentence in full...?

HISTORY
887. ► What were the first and second countries to recognize the State of Israel?

LANGUAGE
888. ► What is the literal meaning of the word *Ashkenaz*?

GEOGRAPHY
889. ► Name one of the two major fortresses constructed by King Solomon...?

ANSWERS

CURRENT
EVENTS
   883. ► General George Brown.

ARTS &
CULTURES
   834. ► The Arabs.

PEOPLE
   885. ► Bobby Fischer.

RELIGION
   836. ► "Love thy neighbor as thyself".

HISTORY
   887. ► The United States and Russia, respectively.

LANGUAGE
   888. ► The section of Europe where Germany is located.

GEOGRAPHY
   889. ► Either "Meggido" or "Hatzor".

CURRENT
EVENTS

890. ► What South American nation publicly condemned Zionism on June 3, 1975, and thus sparked a Jewish boycott of this country?

ARTS &
CULTURES

891. ► This foreign culture was the first to influence the ancient Jewish heritage and mind...?

PEOPLE

892. ► In response to charges of being a Jew, this 19th century English Jewish born politician stated: "Yes, I am a Jew, and when the ancestors of the right honorable gentlemen were brutal savages living in caves, my ancestors were priests in the Temple of Solomon" ...?

RELIGION

893. ► This Biblical figure typifies an anti-Semite more than any other character in the Bible...?

HISTORY

894. ► Name three out of the four greatest powers in Biblical times...?

LANGUAGE

895. ► What does the word *Beth*, used in the names of many Synagogues, mean?

GEOGRAPHY

896. ► The first completely Jewish city in the modern world was...?

ANSWERS

CURRENT
EVENTS **890.** ► **Mexico.**

ARTS &
CULTURES **891.** ► **The Greek.**

PEOPLE **892.** ► **Benjamin Disraeli (in a Parliament debate).**

RELIGION **893.** ► **Haman.**

HISTORY **894.** ► **(Any three of these): Babylon, Persia, Egypt, Assyria.**

LANGUAGE **895.** ► **"House of".**

GEOGRAPHY **896.** ► **Tel Aviv.**

CURRENT
EVENTS

897. ▶ President Carter fired this well-known Jewish co-chairperson of the "National Advisory Committee on Women" and, as a result, half of the organization's members quit...?

ARTS &
CULTURES

898. ▶ This Jewish singer wrote a famous song about a restaurant where one "could get anything you want"...?

PEOPLE

899. ▶ This distinguished Jewish businessman was known as "The Advisor of Presidents"...?

RELIGION

900. ▶ This Biblical book tells the Story of Creation...?

HISTORY

901. ▶ What type of organization was Father Coughlin's Social Justice group, formed in the U.S. in the 1940's?

LANGUAGE

902. ▶ What two Hebrew letters were the original roots of the word "alphabet"?

GEOGRAPHY

903. ▶ In what country was Adolph Eichmann hiding when he was captured by Israeli agents?

ANSWERS

CURRENT
EVENTS

897. ► Bella Abzug.

ARTS &
CULTURES

898. ► Arlo Guthrie ("Alice's Restaurant").

PEOPLE

899. ► Bernard Baruch.

RELIGION

900. ► Genesis.

HISTORY

901. ► Fiercely anti-semitic, preaching hatred towards the Jewish people.

LANGUAGE

902. ► Aleph and Bet. (The concept of the alphabet was created by the ancient Hebrews and brought by them and the Phoenicians to the rest of the world.)

GEOGRAPHY

903. ► Argentina.

CURRENT
EVENTS

904. ► On October 4, 1973, what demands did Arab hijackers make upon the Austrian government, which the Austrians agreed to go along with?

ARTS &
CULTURES

905. ► Which "crazy" Jewish comedian-actor was originally named Joseph Levitch?

PEOPLE

906. ► In ancient Jerusalem, this Ethiopian Queen came to visit a king...?

RELIGION

907. ► Jewish prayer is traditionally conducted facing this direction...?

HISTORY

908. ► There are several major similarities between U.S. and Israeli history. Name three historical parallels...?

LANGUAGE

909. ► What is an *etrog*?

GEOGRAPHY

910. ► After King Solomon died and his Kingdom of Israel was divided in two, what was the capital of the Kingdom of Israel and the Kingdom of Judah?

ANSWERS

904. ► They closed down the Schonau transit camp for Jewish refugees coming from Russia to Israel.

905. ► Jerry Lewis.

906. ► The Queen of Sheba.

907. ► East.

908. ► Both are populated by a diversity of immigrants; both were wildernesses requiring pioneers; both achieved independence from Great Britain; and immigration to both was motivated by the desire to escape persecution and achieve freedom.

909. ► A citron (used during the Succoth holiday).

910. ► Samaria for Israel and Jerusalem for Judah.

CURRENT
EVENTS

911. ► On Sept. 5, 1973, Italian police arrested five Arabs in an apartment near the Rome airport. What spectacular terrorist act were these Arabs planning against an EL AL flight that day?

ARTS &
CULTURES

912. ► This outrageous, self deprecating, Jewish comedienne created the movie *Rabbit Test* about the world's first pregnant man...?

PEOPLE

913. ► Why did Rabbi David Einhorn, a staunch supporter of President Lincoln, have to flee for his life from a Baltimore, Maryland mob, in 1861?

RELIGION

914. ► This prayer is prescribed for those on their deathbeds...?

HISTORY

915. ► This famous Jewish scholar taught the following concept: "Do not judge your fellow man until you put yourself in his place"...?

LANGUAGE

916. ► What does the *Kotel Ma'aravi* refer to?

GEOGRAPHY

917. ► Where is Jericho located, in relation to the Dead Sea?

ANSWERS

911. ► They were planning to shoot the plane down with a Russian SAM-7 missile.

912. ► Joan Rivers.

913. ► Because of his fiery speeches against slavery.

914. ► The "Shema".

915. ► Hillel.

916. ► The Western Wall or the Wailing Wall.

917. ► On the Northwestern coast of the Dead Sea.

CURRENT
EVENTS
    918. ► What are the two types of legal courts found in Israel?

ARTS &
CULTURES
    919. ► This Jewish author wrote *Princess Daisy* and *Scruples*...?

PEOPLE
    920. ► This 15th century Jewish born French doctor was the most famous forecaster in history...?

RELIGION
    921. ► Where is the *Mizrach* physically located in a Synagogue?

HISTORY
    922. ► In WWI, the "Jewish Battalion", otherwise known as the "Zion Mule Corps", fought in this area and under this leader...?

LANGUAGE
    923. ► The *Bimah* in a synagogue refers to this...?

GEOGRAPHY
    924. ► Moses Montefiore built a famous landmark in Jerusalem in the late 1800's, which stands as the Montefiore museum today. What was its original use?

ANSWERS

918. ▶ Civil courts and religious courts.

919. ▶ Judith Krantz.

920. ▶ Nostradamus.

921. ▶ The Eastern wall (the Holy Ark holding the Scrolls of the Law and the pulpit are located there).

922. ▶ They fought in Palestine under the leadership of Zev Jabotinsky.

923. ▶ The raised platform in front of the congregation on which the Rabbi stands.

924. ▶ A windmill (intended to help the early settlers outside the walls of the Old City, grind their grain).

CURRENT
EVENTS

925. ► Issam Sartawi, a P.L.O. moderate who had frequent meetings with Israeli leaders, was assassinated in a Portuguese hotel lobby where the Congress of the Socialist International was meeting. Which extremist group claimed responsibility for the 1983 killing?

ARTS &
CULTURES

926. ► Jewish talent, Boris Thomaschefsky, was renowned in this entertainment discipline...?

PEOPLE

927. ► This Jewish scientist discovered the first polio vaccine...?

RELIGION

928. ► What is the *Mehitza* found mainly in Orthodox synagogues...?

LANGUAGE

929. ► Samuel created a monarchy because...?

LANGUAGE

930. ► The word *Minhag* means...?

GEOGRAPHY

931. ► This place of higher learning, with branches in New York City and Cincinnati, has a School of Archaeology in Jerusalem...?

ANSWERS

CURRENT EVENTS
925. ► The Abu Nidal Palestinian organization.

ARTS & CULTURES
926. ► Acting.

PEOPLE
927. ► Jonas Salk.

RELIGION
928. ► The partition used to separate men and women from one another during religious ceremonies.

HISTORY
929. ► The people wanted a king to unite them against their enemies, so that they could be like other nations.

LANGUAGE
930. ► Ritual (custom).

GEOGRAPHY
931. ► Hebrew Union College.

CURRENT
EVENTS

932. ► How many of the current major Jewish communities are over 100 years old?

ARTS &
CULTURES

933. ► Approximately how many Jews were allowed to emigrate from the Soviet Union in the 1970's?

PEOPLE

934. ► William F. Fulbright, the originator of the scholarship which bears his name, is acknowledged to be the father of this scientific discipline...?

RELIGION

935. ► One of these Biblical brothers was a hunter, the other was a farmer...?

HISTORY

936. ► Which group was responsible for changing the name of Israel to "Palestine"?

LANGUAGE

937. ► The "amud" in a synagogue refers to this...?

GEOGRAPHY

938. ► Within 100 feet, approximately how high is Jerusalem above sea level?

ANSWERS

CURRENT
EVENTS
932. ► **None. All of the major communities were destroyed during the Holocaust.**

ARTS &
CULTURES
933. ► **200,000.**

PEOPLE
934. ► **Archaeology.**

RELIGION
935. ► **Cain and Abel.**

HISTORY
936. ► **The Romans (after they exiled the Jews).**

LANGUAGE
937. ► **The pulpit from which the Rabbi conducts the service.**

GEOGRAPHY
938. ► **1800 feet.**

CURRENT
EVENTS   939. ► The approximate Jewish population of
                       England is...?

ARTS &
CULTURES   940. ► These two Jewish champs, Emanuel
                       Lasker and Wilhelm Steinitz, excelled
                       in this area...?

PEOPLE   941. ► In 1918, Jewish businessman Max
                       Goldberg of Detroit, opened the first
                       one of these. They are indispensable
                       in all large and crowded cities
                       today...?

RELIGION   942. ► The Jewish New Year, or "Rosh
                       Hashanah," has several other names in
                       English. Cite one other name...?

HISTORY   943. ► The "Lesser Sanhedrins" were...?

LANGUAGE   944. ► These Hebrew names – *Ir Hakodesh*
                       and *Ir Hashalom* – refer to the same
                       place, Jerusalem, although they mean
                       different things. What do they mean?

GEOGRAPHY   945. ► What town in Canaan preceded
                       Jerusalem as the main religious center
                       for the Jewish people?

ANSWERS

CURRENT
EVENTS

939. ▶ 420,000.

ARTS &
CULTURES

940. ▶ Chess (they were both world champions).

PEOPLE

941. ▶ Commercial parking lots.

RELIGION

942. ▶ (Any one of these): The first of the Ten Days of Awe; the Day of Remembrance; the Day of the World's Birth.

HISTORY

943. ▶ Ancient provincial courts, assigned to every Jewish town (each with 25 members, appointed by Jerusalem's "Great Sanhedrin").

LANGUAGE

944. ▶ *Ir Hakodesh* means Holy City; *Ir Hashalom* means City of Peace.

GEOGRAPHY

945. ▶ "Shiloh".

CURRENT
EVENTS

946. ► Approximately how many Kibbutzim are there in Israel?

ARTS &
CULTURES

947. ► He is best known as the Jewish journalist that writes books describing Presidential elections...?

PEOPLE

948. ► This Jewish photo-artist is the international superstar of fashion and portrait photography...?

RELIGION

949. ► The smallest book in the Bible, containing only one chapter, is...?

HISTORY

950. ► The Balfour Declaration was signed in this month of this year...?

LANGUAGE

951. ► The Yiddish descriptive expression *Moishe Kapoyer* refers to...?

GEOGRAPHY

952. ► Why is Kishinev notorious in Jewish history?

ANSWERS

946. ► Over 300.

947. ► Theodore White (*The Making of the President* was one of his books).

948. ► Richard Avedon.

949. ► Obadiah.

950. ► November of 1917 (November 2nd).

951. ► A complaining, discontent person.

952. ► It was the site of an infamous *Pogrom*, in 1903.

CURRENT EVENTS

953. ► Currently, what general role does religion play in the government of Israel?

ARTS & CULTURES

954. ► This Jewish editor of *Ms.* Magazine was quoted as saying, "Marriage makes you legally half a person"...?

PEOPLE

955. ► Jerusalem has a street called Orde Circle, named after Orde Wingate. What did he do to deserve this honor?

RELIGION

956. ► The Biblical significance of the location "Moriah" is...?

HISTORY

957. ► What was the historian Josephus Flavius referring to when he described King Herod's great achievement: "He made a mountain of shining gold and lustrous white marble beckoning the pilgrim from afar"...?

LANGUAGE

958. ► The city *Tel Aviv* translates in English to...?

GEOGRAPHY

959. ► In which country was this famous solution to the Jewish problem suggested: "Kill one third, then one third will leave and the rest will convert"...?

ANSWERS

CURRENT EVENTS 953. ▶ Religion is not separated and influences the government. (All government offices and institutions must observe the Sabbath and all Festivals.)

ARTS & CULTURES 954. ▶ Gloria Steinem.

PEOPLE 955. ▶ He was a British officer who actively supported the cause of the Jewish people in Palestine. (He was most active from 1936 to 1939.)

RELIGION 956. ▶ The mountain that the Temple was built upon, and where G-d tested Abraham.

HISTORY 957. ▶ The Second Temple.

LANGUAGE 958. ▶ "Hill of Spring."

GEOGRAPHY 959. ▶ Russia. (This plan was presented to Alexander III by Pobjedonostew, his counselor.)

CURRENT
EVENTS

960. ► What group or groups are in charge of administering and maintaining religious institutions in Jerusalem?

ARTS &
CULTURES

961. ► Jewish musician Jascha Heifetz, is known as a great...?

PEOPLE

962. ► What day was the Jewish psychiatrist Erich Fromm referring to when he said: "This ... is a day of peace between man and nature"?

RELIGION

963. ► The ancient "Abyssinian" Jews are today referred to as...?

HISTORY

964. ► How did the Jews suffer under the U.S. post-World War I immigration laws?

LANGUAGE

965. ► The Biblical word "Jubilee" refers to...?

GEOGRAPHY

966. ► In modern times, this European country has had the highest proportion of Jews in its Senate and Cabinet...?

ANSWERS

CURRENT EVENTS 960. ► Each religion administers its own Holy places.

ARTS & CULTURES 961. ► Violinist.

PEOPLE 962. ► The "Sabbath".

RELIGION 963. ► "Falashas".

HISTORY 964. ► Quotas were established that discriminated against Jews by indirectly limiting the number of immigrants from Eastern Europe and Southern Europe.

LANGUAGE 965. ► The 50th year: or the year of returning land to its original owners; or the freeing of the Hebrew slaves (Leviticus).

GEOGRAPHY 966. ► France.

CURRENT
EVENTS

967. ► Which two American Jewish organizations collect the most money for Israel?

ARTS &
CULTURES

968. ► Sid Luckman, the great Jewish Chicago Bears quarterback, played football for and graduated from this Ivy League school...?

PEOPLE

969. ► This Jewish public servant served in Roosevelt's Cabinet as Secretary of Treasury...?

RELIGION

970. ► The Bible states that the *Messiah* will be a descendant of this Jewish leader...?

HISTORY

971. ► He attempted to annihilate all of the Jews of Arabia...?

LANGUAGE

972. ► The Hebrew expression *vatik* refers to...?

GEOGRAPHY

973. ► What was the most anti-Semitic state in Germany, during the rise of Hitler, prior to World War II?

ANSWERS

967. ► The United Jewish Appeal and Israel Bonds.

968. ► Columbia University.

969. ► Henry Morganthau, Jr.

970. ► King David.

971. ► Mohammed.

972. ► One who settled in Israel before 1948.

973. ► Bavaria.

CURRENT
EVENTS
974. ► These two congregations in New York City, combined to build the largest temple in the world...?

ARTS &
CULTURES
975. ► This Jewish performer is the world's most famous mime...?

PEOPLE
976. ► These three Jewish brothers are best known for their Canadian banking fortune...?

RELIGION
977. ► If an injured party is deceased, how can one who has sinned against the deceased repent on "Yom Kippur"?

HISTORY
978. ► Who overthrew the Jewish Maccabean Kingdom?

LANGUAGE
979. ► What is "Agudath Israel"?

GEOGRAPHY
980. ► Anne Frank and her family hid from the Nazis in this city...?

ANSWERS

CURRENT EVENTS
974. ▶ Temple Emanuel and Temple Beth-El.

ARTS & CULTURES
975. ▶ Marcel Marceau.

PEOPLE
976. ▶ The Belzbergs.

RELIGION
977. ▶ The sinner must go to the burial place and request forgiveness before ten witnesses, in order to be absolved of the sin.

HISTORY
978. ▶ The Romans (in the first century B.C.E.).

LANGUAGE
979. ▶ An international group of strictly Orthodox Jews, who use the Torah to solve all problems confronting Jews.

GEOGRAPHY
980. ▶ Amsterdam.

CURRENT
EVENTS
    981. ► What is the second most common serious genetic disease to affect Jews?

ARTS &
CULTURES
    982. ► This Jewish singer-songwriter was part of a superstar duo group of the 1960's and 1970's, and he starred in the movie *One Trick Pony...*?

PEOPLE
    983. ► In 1944, this Arab leader demanded that the German air force bomb: Tel Aviv, Haifa, Israel's electric generators and more...?

RELIGION
    984. ► The prayer of *Tal* is...?

HISTORY
    985. ► When was the British "Mandate for Palestine" granted by the League of Nations?

LANGUAGE
    986. ► What does the word *Galus* refer to?

GEOGRAPHY
    987. ► This man-made channel connects the Mediterranean to the Red Sea...?

ANSWERS

981. ► Gaucher's Disease.

982. ► Paul Simon.

983. ► The Mufti of Jerusalem (Haj Amin al-Huseyni).

984. ► The prayer for dew (said during Passover).

985. ► 1922.

986. ► Exile or Diasporah.

987. ► The Suez Canal.

CURRENT
EVENTS

988. ▶ In response to this Arab action, a special "Tax Reform Act" was passed by Congress, to deny tax benefit to U.S. businesses participating in the action...?

ARTS &
CULTURES

989. ▶ This Jewish songwriter composed "Over the Rainbow"...?

PEOPLE

990. ▶ This man has been Mayor of Jerusalem longer than any other Mayor...?

RELIGION

991. ▶ What body of laws are memorized by pious Jews?

HISTORY

992. ▶ What was Masada built for?

LANGUAGE

993. ▶ The "Miracle of the Hebrew language" refers to...?

GEOGRAPHY

994. ▶ What are the two major lakes in Israel?

ANSWERS

988. ► The Arab boycott against firms doing business with Israel.

989. ► Harold Arlen.

990. ► Teddy Kollek.

991. ► The "Oral Laws".

992. ► A refuge for King Herod and his family — a royal citadel.

993. ► The survival of Hebrew as a spoken and written language, while all other ancient contemporary languages died.

994. ► Lake Kinneret (Sea of Galilee) and the Dead Sea.

CURRENT
EVENTS
995. ► This city is the home of the Israeli Philharmonic...?

ARTS &
CULTURES
996. ► Jews were distinguished in this profession during the Middle Ages, and are still the most distinguished group in the profession today...?

PEOPLE
997. ► Bernard Baruch was responsible for the most powerful of all wartime government agencies during World War II. What did this agency do?

RELIGION
998. ► Why is the *Chanukah* Festival the most popular and well known Jewish holiday to non-Jews?

HISTORY
999. ► More than one million Jews perished in this ancient siege...?

LANGUAGE
1000. ► The Hebrew word for "Jew" is...?

GEOGRAPHY
1001. ► What city was home to the first Jewish Congregation in Canada?

ANSWERS

995. ► Tel Aviv.

996. ► Medicine.

997. ► The War Industries Board. (It had total command over the entire U.S. production of finished goods and raw materials.)

998. ► Because it occurs so close to the Christian celebration of Christmas.

999. ► The "Siege of Titus."

1000. ► *Yehudi.*

1001. ► Montreal (The "Shearith Israel" Congregation").

CURRENT
EVENTS
1002. ► The most widely read English-language newspaper in Israel is...?

ARTS &
CULTURES
1003. ► Name one of Menachem Begin's two famous books?

PEOPLE
1004. ► He built a merchant fleet during Biblical times, in order to trade with the East...?

RELIGION
1005. ► Name one of the symbolic meanings of the 3-sided *Hamantaschen*, traditionally eaten on *Purim?*

HISTORY
1006. ► What was the main purpose of the legal forum created by the Spanish Inquisition?

LANGUAGE
1007. ► What is Israel's *Adloyada?*

GEOGRAPHY
1008 ► To which city's Jewish congregation did George Washington write his famous letter of religious tolerance and encouragement?

ANSWERS

1002. ► The *Jerusalem Post*.

1003. ► "White Nights" or "The Revolt."

1004. ► King Solomon (Kings II).

1005. ► These 3-sided pastries represent: Haman's 3-sided hat or the 3 people who met to decide the fate of the Jewish people—Esther, Haman and King Ahasuerus.

1006. ► To detect and punish heretics and newly-converted Christians, who practiced Judaism secretly.

1007. ► A *Purim* Carnival Parade.

1008. ► The Congregation of Newport, R.I.

CURRENT
EVENTS   **1009.** ► On which fronts was Israel attacked at the beginning of the Yom Kippur War?

ARTS &
CULTURES   **1010.** ► This Jewish slugger of the 1930's and 1940's had 331 career home runs, including 11 grand slams...?

PEOPLE   **1011.** ► Why did Judah Benjamin, a famous Jewish statesman, leave the U.S. after the Civil War, moving to England?

RELIGION   **1012.** ► Who was originally being referred to in the Biblical expression: "Thrown into the lion's den"...?

HISTORY   **1013.** ► This leader arranged for a *Sanhedrin* in the 19th century.

LANGUAGE   **1014.** ► Who were the *Kedoshim*?

GEOGRAPHY   **1015.** ► On what body of water is the city of Tiberias located?

ANSWERS

CURRENT
EVENTS 1009. ► On the Egyptian front (the Sinai), and on the Syrian front (the Golan Heights).

ARTS &
CULTURES 1010. ► Hank Greenberg.

PEOPLE 1011. ► Because he served in the government of the Confederacy and was held responsible for some of the South's losses.

RELIGION 1012. ► Daniel.

HISTORY 1013. ► Napoleon.

LANGUAGE 1014. ► Jews who died for their religion, during periods of persecution throughout history.

GEOGRAPHY 1015. ► The Sea of Galilee.

CURRENT
EVENTS   1016. ► Who initiated the concept of "Shuttle Diplomacy," and what was his title?

ARTS &
CULTURES   1017. ► This Jewish artist's work prominently decorates the United Nations...?

PEOPLE   1018. ► The real name of Achad Haam is...?

RELIGION   1019. ► What are the divisions among the prophets?

HISTORY   1020. ► How did President Lincoln demonstrate his support and friendship to the Jews of America, in response to an anti-Semitic government incident?

LANGUAGE   1021. ► The location known as *Migdal David* translates to...?

GEOGRAPHY   1022. ► A special garden has been planted in Jerusalem bearing the names of this courageous special group of Gentiles...?.

ANSWERS

CURRENT EVENTS **1016.** ► Henry Kissinger, U.S. Secretary of State.

ARTS & CULTURES **1017.** ► Marc Chagall.

PEOPLE **1018.** ► Asher Ginzberg.

RELIGION **1019.** ► They are divided into Major and Minor Prophets.

HISTORY **1020.** ► He told a delegation of Jews that he disagreed with General Grant's order expelling Jews from certain areas.

LANGUAGE **1021.** ► The Tower of David.

GEOGRAPHY **1022.** ► "Righteous Gentiles"—for those who risked their lives to help save Jews during the Nazi era.

CURRENT
EVENTS
1023. ► What percentage of U.S. Jews live in large metropolitan areas?

ARTS &
CULTURES
1024. ► This distinguished Washington museum is famous for its architecture...?

PEOPLE
1025. ► Why was Lot's wife turned into a pillar of salt?

RELIGION
1026. ► At Orthodox weddings, the bride circles the groom how many times?

HISTORY
1027. ► Why was Jezebel considered evil?

LANGUAGE
1028. ► What was the famous "Mortara case" of 1958 Italy?

GEOGRAPHY
1029. ► What does Israel's "Ha-Mossad" translate in English to?

ANSWERS

CURRENT EVENTS 1023. ► Ninety-five percent.

ARTS & CULTURES 1024. ► The Joseph Hirshorn Museum.

PEOPLE 1025. ► She looked back at the destruction of Sodom.

RELIGION 1026. ► Seven.

HISTORY 1027. ► A dispute over the possession of a Jewish child, kidnapped by a Catholic nurse, baptized by the Church, and withheld successfully from the Jewish parents.

LANGUAGE 1028. ► The Institute. (It refers to Israel's counter-intelligence service.)

GEOGRAPHY 1029. ► 1300 feet.

CURRENT
EVENTS   1030. ► In Israel, what type of court cases, if
                any, are heard by a jury?

ARTS &
CULTURES   1031. ► Name any three musical instruments
                referred to in the Bible...?

PEOPLE   1032. ► He conceived the first Zionist Con-
                gress in Basle, Switzerland, in 1897...?

RELIGION   1033. ► What prophet objected to the violation
                of Jewish laws, introduced by King
                Ahab and Queen Jezebel, and warned
                that the kingdom would be destroyed?

HISTORY   1034. ► After World War I, the "Balfour
                Declaration" was made a part of this
                peace treaty...?

LANGUAGE   1035. ► The Hebrew word for "charity" is...?

GEOGRAPHY   1036. ► Approximately how many miles is
                Jerusalem from Tel Aviv?

ANSWERS

CURRENT
EVENTS **1030.** ► **None. Israel does not have a jury system.**

ARTS &
CULTURES **1031.** ► **(Any three of these): Horn, pipe, timbrel, harp, cymbals.**

PEOPLE **1032.** ► **Dr. Theodore Herzl.**

RELIGION **1033.** ► **Elijah.**

HISTORY **1034.** ► **The peace treaty between the Allies and Turkey.**

LANGUAGE **1035.** ► *Tzedakah.*

GEOGRAPHY **1036.** ► **Forty-four miles.**

CURRENT
EVENTS

1037. ▶ The members of England's Parliament are called M.P.'s. What abbreviation is used for members of Israel's Parliament?

ARTS &
CULTURES

1038. ▶ Jewish sports enthusiast Hirsch Jacobs was famous for his skill and knowledge in this specialized area of racing...?

PEOPLE

1039. ▶ This king was described in the Bible as being a giant, with a bed 9 cubits long and 4 cubits wide...?

RELIGION

1040. ▶ This Biblical book belongs to Israel's Persian period...?

HISTORY

1041. ▶ What type of legal forum was created by the Spanish Inquisition?

LANGUAGE

1042. ▶ For approximately how many years has the Hebrew language been used?

GEOGRAPHY

1043. ▶ This famous Israeli forest is known as *Ya-ar Hak doshim*. What does it mean and why was it created?

ANSWERS

CURRENT EVENTS   1037. ► M.K.s (Members of Knesset).

ARTS & CULTURES   1038. ► Training and breeding of race horses.

PEOPLE   1039. ► King Og (of Bashan). (Deuteronomy.)

RELIGION   1040. ► The Book of Esther.

HISTORY   1041. ► A court (set up by Ferdinand and Isabella, to route out and punish heretics and Marranos).

LANGUAGE   1042. ► Four thousand years.

GEOGRAPHY   1043. ► The Forest of the Martyrs, memorializing the six million Jewish victims of the Holocaust.

CURRENT
EVENTS   **1044.** ► The two major Israeli political parties are...?

ARTS &
CULTURES   **1045.** ► *The Man Who Saw Tomorrow* was a 1982 movie narrated by Orson Welles, about the prophecies of this French Jewish born, self-acclaimed prophet of the 15th century...?

PEOPLE   **1046.** ► He had 1,000 wives, according to the Book of Kings...?

RELIGION   **1047.** ► What is the oldest known holiday in Western Civilization that has been continuously observed?

HISTORY   **1048.** ► This country took control of Palestine after the collapse of the Ottoman Empire...?

LANGUAGE   **1049.** ► This type of Israeli settlement included both cooperative as well as private ownership...?

GEOGRAPHY   **1050.** ► Approximately what percentage of Israeli Jews were born in Israel?

ANSWERS

1044. ► *Labor* and *Heruth*.

1045. ► Nostradamus.

1046. ► Solomon.

1047. ► Passover.

1048. ► Great Britain.

1049. ► A *moshav*.

1050. ► Fifty-six percent.

CURRENT
EVENTS

1051. ► This Israeli leader said: "We will win because we must live. Our neighbors are fighting not for their lives, not for their sovereignty, they are fighting to destroy us. We will not be destroyed. We dare not be destroyed....The spirit of our people hates war but knows that in order to live it must win the war...forced upon us."...?

ARTS &
CULTURES

1052. ► *Latkes* are eaten on this holiday...?

PEOPLE

1053. ► Dr. Chaim Weizmann, the famous Zionist, first achieved prominence as a scientist in what field...?

RELIGION

1054. ► What was the Biblical event that symbolized the dove and the olive leaf as synonymous with peace?

HISTORY

1055. ► "The Protocols of the Elders of Zion" were...?

LANGUAGE

1056. ► When a *dreidel* lands on the side that reads *hay* the player is entitled to...?

GEOGRAPHY

1057. ► During World War I, in what region of the world did the Jewish people suffer the most?

ANSWERS

1051. ► Golda Meir (Oct. 13th, 1973).

1052. ► *Chanukah*.

1053. ► Chemistry.

1054. ► The dove returned to Noah's ark with an olive leaf, signaling that the water had subsided.

1055. ► An anti-Semitic document that alleged an international Jewish plan to take over the world. (Henry Ford publicized and referred to this as the basis of his anti-Semitic propaganda.)

1056. ► "Take half" (or *halb*).

1057. ► Eastern Europe (the Russian and German armies fought one another with the Jews in between).

CURRENT
EVENTS

1058. ► This Jewish public servant resigned from his post as U.S. Representative to the United Nations in 1968, due to a disagreement with President Johnson's Vietnam policy...?

ARTS &
CULTURES

1059. ► What German Jewish-born author said: "Where they burn books, they burn people," 100 years before Hitler came to power?

PEOPLE

1060. ► This Jewish scientist invented the second polio vaccine, which could be taken orally...?

RELIGION

1061. ► What famous Biblical passage is written on the Liberty Bell...?

HISTORY

1062. ► What was the reasoning behind the anti-Semitism encouraged by Russia's Czarist governments, and the consistent persecution of their Jewish population?

LANGUAGE

1063. ► What is a *Keter Torah*?

GEOGRAPHY

1064. ► The Galveston Movement, beginning after World War I, was started to...?

ANSWERS

CURRENT EVENTS   1058. ► Arthur Goldberg.

ARTS & CULTURES   1059. ► Heinrich Heine.

PEOPLE   1060. ► Albert Sabin.

RELIGION   1061. ► "Proclaim Liberty throughout the land, unto all the inhabitants thereof."

HISTORY   1062. ► To preoccupy the masses with something other than the dissatisfaction with their leadership.

LANGUAGE   1063. ► A "Torah crown."

GEOGRAPHY   1064. ► Redirect the massive Jewish-American immigration from the crowded Eastern cities to the agricultural areas of the South and Southwest, using Galveston, Texas as the stopping off point.

CURRENT
EVENTS

1065. ► Who was the partially Jewish presidential candidate who ran for office after 1956, but before 1976?

ARTS &
CULTURES

1066. ► He was known as the "Jewish Mark Twain" and his real name was Solomon Rabinowitz...?

PEOPLE

1067. ► This public servant of the Land of Israel said: "No State is handed to a people on a silver platter."...?

RELIGION

1068. ► This Jewish religious ceremony began in the 14th century, and is even more popular today among Jewish families?

HISTORY

1069. ► What clandestine Jewish organization was the basis for the Israeli Army?

LANGUAGE

1070. ► The *Hamotzi* prayer is said over...?

GEOGRAPHY

1071. ► What was the last independent nation in Palestine before the creation of the modern State of Israel?

ANSWERS

1065. ▶ **Barry Goldwater.**

1066. ▶ **Sholem Aleichem.**

1067. ▶ **Chaim Weitzmann.**

1068. ▶ **The *Bar Mitzvah*.**

1069. ▶ **The *Hagannah*.**

1070. ▶ **Bread.**

1071. ▶ **Ancient Israel.**

CURRENT
EVENTS   1072. ► What issue are all Israelis united on?

ARTS &
CULTURES   1073. ► The ancient Jewish historian Josephus Flavius wrote this classic work, explaining the history of the Jews from the beginning of time through Nero's reign. . .?

PEOPLE   1074. ► This Biblical figure lived longer than any other. . .?

RELIGION   1075. ► According to the *Mishna*, what is the proper age for a Jew to marry?

HISTORY   1076. ► According to the Bible, how did only Jonathan and his armor-bearer defeat an entire Philistine army?

LANGUAGE   1077. ► The English term "behemoth" refers to. . .?

GEOGRAPHY   1078. ► What country instituted the anti-Semitic "May Laws"?

ANSWERS

CURRENT
EVENTS
    1072. ► Defending themselves against a common enemy intent upon their destruction.

ARTS &
CULTURES
    1073. ► "Antiquities of the Jews."

PEOPLE
    1074. ► Methuselah.

RELIGION
    1075. ► Eighteen.

HISTORY
    1076. ► They boldly approached the Philistine army, bluffing them into believing there was an Israelite army following behind them.

LANGUAGE
    1077. ► In English it means a large animal or something that is monstrously huge or powerful. (In Hebrew it means cow.)

GEOGRAPHY
    1078. ► Russia (in 1811).

CURRENT EVENTS   1079. ► Rabbi Baruch Korff was famous for his unending support for what or whom?

ARTS & CULTURES   1080. ► This Jewish author wrote two novels on the historic figures Michelangelo and Vincent Van Gogh...?

PEOPLE   1081. ► This Jewish man of science said: "Whatever we do for ... Israel we do for the honor and well-being of the whole Jewish people"...?

RELIGION   1082. ► *Tefillin* are wrapped around the arm how many times?

HISTORY   1083. ► When the Nazis demanded that all Jews wear yellow identification stars, the ruler of this country wore a star himself and the entire population followed his lead, thus circumventing the Nazis, and saving many Jewish lives...?

LANGUAGE   1084. ► The Hebrew word *Gehenom* refers to...?

GEOGRAPHY   1085. ► What Chinese city was home to 20,000 European Jewish refugees during World War II?

ANSWERS

1079. ► Richard Nixon.

1080. ► Irving Stone (*The Agony and the
Ecstasy* and *Lust for Life*).

PEOPLE 1081. ► Albert Einstein.

RELIGION 1082. ► Seven.

HISTORY 1083. ► The King of Denmark.

LANGUAGE 1084. ► The hell-like valley of Hinnom, near
Jerusalem (used for garbage disposal
and child sacrifices by the Heathens).

GEOGRAPHY 1085. ► Shanghai.

CURRENT
EVENTS   1086. ► Approximately what percentage of world Jewry currently lives in Israel?

ARTS &
CULTURES   1087. ► Shlomo Carlebach is popularly referred to as...?

PEOPLE   1088. ► The results of this medieval marriage, arranged by Jewish bankers, was later to cause much suffering among the Jews...?

RELIGION   1089. ► In the Bible, who said: "I am that I am"...?

HISTORY   1090. ► Before the destruction of the Second Temple by the Romans, what was the approximate Jewish population in Palestine?

LANGUAGE   1091. ► The Jewish people have maintained an allegiance to the Hebrew language for thousands of years. The main benefit has been...?

GEOGRAPHY   1092. ► What is the oldest synagogue in America, that is still standing today?

ANSWERS

CURRENT EVENTS	**1086.** ► Twenty-five percent.
ARTS & CULTURES	**1087.** ► "The Dancing Rabbi."
PEOPLE	**1088.** ► King Ferdinand (of Aragon) and Queen Isabella (of Castillo).
RELIGION	**1089.** ► G-d (speaking to Moses).
HISTORY	**1090.** ► Between five and six million (according to Josephus Flavius, the historian).
LANGUAGE	**1091.** ► The preservation of cultural uniqueness, and the prevention of complete assimilation while in the Diaspora.
GEOGRAPHY	**1092.** ► The Touro Synagogue, in Newport, Rhode Island.

CURRENT
EVENTS

1093. ► He was Prime Minister of Israel during the Six-Day War...?

ARTS &
CULTURES

1094. ► Jewish artist George Segal is known as a talented...?

PEOPLE

1095. ► Yigael Yadin distinguished himself as a great man in both of his careers. What were they?

RELIGION

1096. ► The main reference book for followers of the *Kabbalah* is...?

HISTORY

1097. ► What were the "Special Night Squads"?

LANGUAGE

1098. ► What was the strike force of the *Haganah* called?

GEOGRAPHY

1099. ► In 1144, where did the first "ritual murder" charge against the Jewish population take place?

ANSWERS

CURRENT
EVENTS 1093. ▶ Levi Eshkol.

ARTS &
CULTURES 1094. ▶ Sculptor.

PEOPLE 1095. ▶ Military officer (he was Israel's second chief of staff) and archaeologist (among other accomplishments, he explored Hazor and Masada).

RELIGION 1096. ▶ The *Zohar*.

HISTORY 1097. ▶ They were special *Haganah* commando units established by the British officer Charles Orde Wingate to protect against Arab terrorist groups in the late 1930's.

LANGUAGE 1098. ▶ *Palmach*.

GEOGRAPHY 1099. ▶ England (Norwich).

CURRENT
EVENTS   1100. ► The approximate Jewish population of
                the U.S. is...?

ARTS &
CULTURES   1101. ► This type of art is the medium of
                famous Jewish artist Jacob Epstein...?

PEOPLE   1102. ► In 1910, Louis Blaustein and his son
                Jacob opened the first one of these, in
                Baltimore...?

RELIGION   1103. ► The synagogue was developed during
                this period as a place of worship...?

HISTORY   1104. ► How many years after the destruction
                of the Temple did Masada fall?

LANGUAGE   1105. ► The Yiddish word *averah* means...?

GEOGRAPHY   1106. ► Jerusalem is located in these hills...?

ANSWERS

CURRENT
EVENTS   **1100.** ► **Six million.**

ARTS &
CULTURES   **1101.** ► **Sculpture.**

PEOPLE   **1102.** ► **Gas station.**

RELIGION   **1103.** ► **The Babylonian exile (which created a
            need for a place of worship due to the
            destruction of the Temple).**

HISTORY   **1104.** ► **Three years.**

LANGUAGE   **1105.** ► **Sin.**

GEOGRAPHY   **1106.** ► **The Judean Hills.**

CURRENT
EVENTS

1107. ► What was the terrorist Abu Daoud's most notorious act?

ARTS &
CULTURES

1108. ► This Jewish cartoonist is famous for hiding his daughter's name in each cartoon...?

PEOPLE

1109. ► Enzio Sereni and Hannah Senesch both distinguished themselves by undergoing this same dangerous mission during World War II...?

RELIGION

1110. ► What does the *Chanukah* celebration prescribe for the performance of work during this holiday?

HISTORY

1111. ► Who was the Roman governor who led the battle against Masada?

LANGUAGE

1112. ► How many letters are there in the Hebrew alphabet?

GEOGRAPHY

1113. ► Approximately what percentage of Israeli Jews were born in Europe and the Americas?

ANSWERS

CURRENT
EVENTS

1107. ► The 1972 Munich Olympic Massacre.

ARTS &
CULTURES

1108. ► Al Hirschfeld (his daughter's name is Nina).

PEOPLE

1109. ► They parachuted behind German lines to help Jewish refugees. (Sereni successfully went to Italy and Senesch went to Hungary, where she was captured and tortured to death.)

RELIGION

1110. ► There is no prohibition against working during *Chanukah*.

HISTORY

1111. ► Flavius Silva.

LANGUAGE

1112. ► Twenty-two.

GEOGRAPHY

1113. ► Twenty-five percent.

CURRENT
EVENTS   1114. ► This Jewish public servant was in President Carter's "Inner Circle," and the head of the Domestic Policy staff...?

ARTS &
CULTURES   1115. ► Jewish musical talent Eugene Ormandy is known as a great..?

PEOPLE   1116. ► This great king of the Jewish people led the reconstruction of the Second Temple...?

RELIGION   1117. ► Who are defined as crypto-Jews?

HISTORY   1118. ► The Joint Distribution Committee was formed after World War I for the purpose of...?

LANGUAGE   1119. ► What was the historic and linguistic symbolism in the name Maccabees?

GEOGRAPHY   1120. ► Israel is located between these two seas...?

ANSWERS

CURRENT
EVENTS   1114. ► Stuart Eizenstat.

ARTS &
CULTURES   1115. ► Conductor.

PEOPLE   1116. ►, "Herod the Great."

RELIGION   1117. ► Those that practice their religion in secret due to religious persecution.

HISTORY   1118. ► Distributing the money that many Jewish organizations collected to help Jewish sufferers of World War I.

LANGUAGE   1119. ► It is an acronym for the Hebrew words: *Mi Kamocha Ba'Elim* or "Who can measure up to You, G-d?"

GEOGRAPHY   1120. ► The Red Sea and the Mediterranean.

CURRENT
EVENTS

1121. ► The number of Jews living in the New York City metropolitan area is approximately...?

ARTS &
CULTURES

1122. ► This Jewish first-time-movie-director directed *Yentl*.

PEOPLE

1123. ► This public servant of the land of Israel said: "We will fight against Hitler as if there is no White Paper and we will fight against the White Paper as if there were no war"...?

RELIGION

1124. ► What is the reason for the "Fast of Esther"?

HISTORY

1125. ► This French leader was the first to improve conditions for the Jews of Europe...?

LANGUAGE

1126. ► The word *dayenu*, spoken during the Passover Seder, means...?

GEOGRAPHY

1127. ► In what special cemetery was the British military Commander Sir Orde Wingate, the great friend of the Jewish population in Israel (before statehood), buried?

ANSWERS

CURRENT EVENTS 1121. ► 2.2 million.

ARTS & CULTURES 1122. ► Barbra Streisand.

PEOPLE 1123. ► David Ben Gurion.

RELIGION 1124. ► It commemorates Queen Esther's fast and prayer before she asked the king to save the Jews from Haman's massacre.

HISTORY 1125. ► Napoleon.

LANGUAGE 1126. ► It would have been sufficient for us.

GEOGRAPHY 1127. ► At Arlington National Cemetery, in Virginia.

CURRENT
EVENTS   **1128.** ► Describe the animal and the type of tree depicted on the emblem of Jerusalem...?

ARTS &
CULTURES   **1129.** ► This Jewish artist's work prominently decorates the Paris Opera House...?

PEOPLE   **1130.** ► This famous Jewish financier-to-be founded the House of Rothschild...?

RELIGION   **1131.** ► Which ancient king addressed his Jewish population and said: "Whosoever there is among you of all his people—the lord his G-d be with him—let him go"...?

HISTORY   **1132.** ► Which Israeli Prime Minister served more than one nonconsecutive term as Prime Minister?

LANGUAGE   **1133.** ► The Jewish wedding canopy is known as...?

GEOGRAPHY   **1134.** ► This was the first country in modern Jewish history where the Jewish population attempted to adapt to the culture and customs of the new land...?

ANSWERS

CURRENT EVENTS **1128. ▶ A lion and olive tree branches.**

ARTS & CULTURES **1129. ▶ Marc Chagall.**

PEOPLE **1130. ▶ Maier Rothschild.**

RELIGION **1131. ▶ Cyrus (He said this to the Jews of Persia, allowing them to return and rebuild Jerusalem).**

HISTORY **1132. ▶ David Ben Gurion (first P.M., 1948–1954 and third P.M., 1955–1962).**

LANGUAGE **1133. ▶ *Chupah*.**

GEOGRAPHY **1134. ▶ Germany.**

CURRENT
EVENTS

1135. ► Who was designated by the President of Israel to form a new government immediately following the July 1984 elections?

ARTS &
CULTURES

1136. ► Jewish author Herman Wouk wrote one of the most famous novels set in World War II, which was later made into a movie starring Humphrey Bogart, Fred McMurray and Jose Ferrer. What was its title?

PEOPLE

1137. ► What man built R.H. Macy into the largest department store in the world...?

RELIGION

1138. ► The *Kaddish* is read for how many months after a death?

HISTORY

1139. ► He was the greatest general in the Bible...?

LANGUAGE

1140. ► The Yiddish expression *sitsfleisch* refers to this quality?

GEOGRAPHY

1141. ► Samuel Doe, president of an African nation, visited Israel in August of 1982, and was the first black leader to arrive for an official visit in more than 10 years. Of what country was he president?

ANSWERS

1135. ► Shimon Peres (of the Labor Party).

1136. ► *The Caine Mutiny*.

1137. ► Isadore and Nathan Straus, of Abraham and Straus (who became sole owners of Macy's in 1896).

1138. ► Eleven.

1139. ► Joshua.

1140. ► Perseverence, especially relating to scholarly studies.

1141. ► Liberia.

CURRENT
EVENTS
1142. ► James Keegstra, an anti-Semitic high school leader in Alberta, Canada and mayor of his village, taught his class that Jews are the root of all evil in the world, and he made one even more outrageous claim. What was this other widely reported lie that he taught his class?

ARTS &
CULTURES
1143. ► This hilarious Jewish comedian-actor-musician was born with the name Allan Stewart Koenigsberg...?

PEOPLE
1144. ► What was Israel's "Operation Ship to Shore"?

RELIGION
1145. ► What is another English name for Pentecost?

HISTORY
1146. ► The Jewish period of prosperity in Spain became known as...?

LANGUAGE
1147. ► The holiday food *kishkeh* is otherwise known by this name...?

GEOGRAPHY
1148. ► The Jewish Theological Seminary of America is located in...?

ANSWERS

CURRENT
EVENTS

1142. ► That the Holocaust never happened.

ARTS &
CULTURES

1143. ► Woody Allen.

PEOPLE

1144. ► The resettlement of refugees in Israel—from their embarkation in Europe to their unloading in Israel.

RELIGION

1145. ► "The Day of the Giving of the Law" or the "Feast of Weeks" (*Shavuoth*).

HISTORY

1146. ► The Golden Age.

LANGUAGE

1147. ► Stuffed derma.

GEOGRAPHY

1148. ► New York City.

CURRENT
EVENTS
    1149. ► What action, if any, did the European economic community take in response to Israel's involvement in the war in Lebanon?

ARTS &
CULTURES
    1150. ► What drink is popularly known as "the Liquor of Israel"?

PEOPLE
    1151. ► He became king of the Jews with the help of the Romans in 37 B.C.E....?

RELIGION
    1152. ► Which holiday festival uses citrons and palm branches?

HISTORY
    1153. ► When did the first Jews arrive in New York?

LANGUAGE
    1154. ► This special meat and bean dish is considered a traditional Sabbath food.

GEOGRAPHY
    1155. ► Where is the largest Jewish house of worship in the United States, and what is its name?

ANSWERS

1149. ► They imposed economic sanctions
(which were lifted a few months
later).

1150. ► Sabra (an orange-chocolate liquor).

1151. ► Herod.

1152. ► "The Feast of Tabernacles" (*Succoth*).

1153. ► In 1654.

1154. ► Cholent.

1155. ► Temple Emanuel, located in New York
City.

CURRENT
EVENTS

1156. ► In Brussels, what happened after *Rosh Hashanah* in September 1982, that shocked the world's Jewish communities?

ARTS &
CULTURES

1157. ► This Jewish educator founded the Ethical Culture Society...?

PEOPLE

1158. ► Who founded Yeshiva University?

RELIGION

1159. ► What Biblical family did Moses put in charge of the Altar and Sanctuary?

HISTORY

1160. ► What approximate percentage of donations to the Jewish Agency were collected in the U.S.A.?

LANGUAGE

1161. ► The Yiddish word *fin* refers to this unit of measure...?

GEOGRAPHY

1162. ► Isaac Stern, the famous Jewish violinist, was born in this country...?

ANSWERS

1156. ► A terrorist fired a machine gun into crowds in front of the city's main synagogue.

ARTS & CULTURES 1157. ► Dr. Felix Adler.

PEOPLE 1158. ► Rabbi Bernard Revel.

RELIGION 1159. ► Aaron's family.

HISTORY 1160. ► Sixty-five percent.

LANGUAGE 1161. ► "Five" or a "Fiver," in reference to money (five dollars).

GEOGRAPHY 1162. ► The United States of America.

CURRENT
EVENTS   1163. ► Which Black Panther, after living in Algeria, recently reversed his anti-Semitic views and became pro-Jewish in his public pronouncements?

ARTS &
CULTURES   1164. ► Theodore Bikel is known as a great Jewish...?

PEOPLE   1165. ► This American Jewish financier was instrumental in organizing the Federal Reserve Board...?

RELIGION   1166. ► What is the original source of the saying: "Cleanliness is next to godliness"?

HISTORY   1167. ► What was the official excuse for limiting immigration to post-World War I Palestine?

LANGUAGE   1168. ► This early Israeli settlement was symbolically named *Petach Tikvah* in 1898. It means...?

GEOGRAPHY   1169. ► Palestine is part of the Middle East as well as this section of the world...?

ANSWERS

1163. ► **Eldridge Cleaver.**

1164. ► **Folk singer.**

1165. ► **Paul M. Warburg.**

1166. ► **The Talmud.**

1167. ► **The British would only allow as many people "as the economic capacity of the country would allow."**

1168. ► **"Gateway of Hope."**

1169. ► **Asia Minor.**

CURRENT
EVENTS

1170. ► He was the only charismatic Jewish mayor of an American city to have written a best selling book...?

ARTS &
CULTURES

1171. ► What is the name of the 1983 movie where Woody Allen offers a stunning critique of Jewish assimilation by giving us a character who is a human chameleon, a man who takes on the mental and physical characteristics of whoever he is with, just so he will be liked...?

PEOPLE

1172. ► This Jewish physicist won the Nobel Prize in 1922, for his work on the structure of the atom...?

RELIGION

1173. ► What perplexed the Biblical figure Job?

HISTORY

1174. ► What was the recognized "Jewish Agency" at the time of the "British Mandate" over Palestine?

LANGUAGE

1175. ► *Maoz Tzur* is sung on this Jewish holiday...?

GEOGRAPHY

1176. ► The names of the 5 Philistine cities referred to in the Bible are still used in Israel today. Name two of them...?

ANSWERS

CURRENT EVENTS   **1170.** ► **Mayor Edward Koch of New York City.**

ARTS & CULTURES   **1171.** ► *Zelig.*

PEOPLE   **1172.** ► **Niels Bohr.**

RELIGION   **1173.** ► **The suffering of the righteous and the prosperity of the wicked.**

HISTORY   **1174.** ► **The Zionist Organization.**

LANGUAGE   **1175.** ► *Chanukah.*

GEOGRAPHY   **1176.** ► **(Any two of these): Ashkelon, Ashdod, Ekron, Gat and Gaza.**

CURRENT
EVENTS

1177. ► In Rome, what happened after *Simchat Torah* services in October 1982, that shocked the civilized world?

ARTS &
CULTURES

1178. ► Joseph Pulitzer is remembered for the prize in journalism which bears his name, but he originally became famous as a newspaper publisher. Can you name either of his two newspapers?

PEOPLE

1179. ► Once known as the world's greatest reporter, he was the first winner of the Pulitzer Prize. He exposed the practice of the Ku Klux Klan in Florida, and became executive editor of the *New York World* in 1920. Who was he?

RELIGION

1180. ► What is the *Ne'ila* prayer?

HISTORY

1181. ► What world organization is B'nai B'rith fashioned after?

LANGUAGE

1182. ► The Yiddish word *Glitch* means this in English...?

GEOGRAPHY

1183. ► The famous Jewish university named after Supreme Court Justice Louis Brandeis is located in this city...?

ANSWERS

1177. ▶ Terrorists fired machine guns and threw hand grenades at crowds in front of Rome's main synagogue.

1178. ▶ The *New York World* or *The St. Louis Post-Dispatch*.

1179. ▶ Henry Bayard Swope.

1180. ▶ The final prayer said on *Yom Kippur*.

1181. ▶ The Free Masons.

1182. ▶ A mechanical defect.

1183. ▶ Waltham, Massachusetts.

CURRENT
EVENTS

1184. ► In December of 1977, El Al began direct flights to this nation for the first time...?

ARTS &
CULTURES

1185. ► This successful T.V. producer based the show *All in the Family* on his father's conservatism, and the show *Maude* on his mother's liberalism...?

PEOPLE

1186. ► What significant unlikely achievement did the Polish Jew Oswald Rufeisen accomplish during World War II, in occupied territory?

RELIGION

1187. ► What is the major theme of the Jewish Reconstructionist Movement?

HISTORY

1188. ► This Jewish leader led a war of freedom from 132 C.E. to 135 C.E. which restored Jerusalem as the Jewish capital...?

LANGUAGE

1189. ► What does *Gan Eden* refer to?

GEOGRAPHY

1190. ► In 1624, the first Jewish settlement in the Western hemisphere was established here...?

ANSWERS

CURRENT EVENTS 1184. ► Egypt.

ARTS & CULTURES 1185. ► Norman Lear.

PEOPLE 1186. ► He managed to become a Nazi officer and secretly helped other Jews, at the same time.

RELIGION 1187. ► Judaism should focus on the needs of this world, instead of the world to come.

HISTORY 1188. ► Bar Kochba.

LANGUAGE 1189. ► The "Garden of Eden".

GEOGRAPHY 1190. ► In Brazil (the town of Bahia).

CURRENT
EVENTS

1191. ► This war was a reaction to Arab threats and blockades and involved Egyptian, Jordanian and Syrian armies?

ARTS &
CULTURES

1192. ► This famous early 20th century Yiddish actor, was considered the world's greatest interpreter of Shakespeare's Shylock...?

PEOPLE

1193. ► Which recent Jewish Presidential Press Secretary was originally named Ronald Nessenbaum?

RELIGION

1194. ► From what Jewish religious book does this quote come from: "Kingdoms arise and Kingdoms pass away, but Israel endures forever"?

HISTORY

1195. ► What is the moral of the "Purim" celebration?

LANGUAGE

1196. ► When a Jew living in Israel goes on *Yerida* it means...?

GEOGRAPHY

1197. ► Between World War I and World War II this continent had the second largest Jewish population...?

ANSWERS

CURRENT
EVENTS

1191. ► The 1967 Six-Day War.

ARTS &
CULTURES

1192. ► Jacob Adler.

PEOPLE

1193. ► Ron Nessen (Press Secretary to President Gerald Ford).

RELIGION

1194. ► The "Midrash".

HISTORY

1195. ► It commemorates the repeated failures throughout history, of the neverending attempts to destroy the Jewish people.

LANGUAGE

1196. ► One has decided to emigrate and "descend".

GEOGRAPHY

1197. ► The American Continent.

CURRENT
EVENTS   1198. ► What did the West German government do with the three Arab terrorists
held for the murder of the Israeli athletes, at the 1972 Munich Olympics?

ARTS &
CULTURES   1199. ► What is the most divisive view of the
hard-core extremist Orthodox move-
ment, concerning Israel...?

PEOPLE   1200. ► He advised President Roosevelt and
other Presidents on economic prob-
lems; planned most of the New Deal
legislation; and was the U.S. representative to the U.N. Atomic Energy
Commission?

RELIGION   1201. ► Which Commandment orders the
keeping of the "Sabbath"?

HISTORY   1202. ► What is the *Golem* made out of, according to legend?

LANGUAGE   1203. ► Who were the *Bilu*?

GEOGRAPHY   1204. ► Where does Israel's "Chanukah Torch
Relay" begin and end?

ANSWERS

1198. ▶ They were released in exchange for a Lufthansa plane, hijacked from Beirut.

1199. ▶ That the creation of Israel is not legitimate until the "Messiah" arrives.

1200. ▶ Bernard Baruch.

1201. ▶ The fourth.

1202. ▶ Clay.

1203. ▶ The first settlers from Russia (arriving in Palestine in 1882).

1204. ▶ It begins in Modiin (hometown of the Macabees) and continues to Jerusalem (where the torch lights a giant Menorah).

Trivia Judaica™   **QUESTIONS**

CURRENT EVENTS

1205. ► In 1977, Yitzhak Rabin's government was not on good terms with this Israeli political party which eventually decided to join the Likud coalition...?

ARTS & CULTURES

1206. ► This Jewish showman created a famous, still remembered, American burlesque show...?

PEOPLE

1207. ► He was a physician and a philosopher on Jewish Laws and Jewish thinking. He wrote the *Mishneh Torah* and the *Guide for the Perplexed*...?

RELIGION

1208. ► Why does the Bible command the Israelites to treat "Strangers and Foreigners" at their gates, with "Kindness and Justice"...?

HISTORY

1209. ► When King Solomon was building the First Temple, where did he get the cedar wood and the know-how to construct the project?

LANGUAGE

1210. ► The word "Deuteronomy" means...?

GEOGRAPHY

1211. ► The "Mandelbaum Gate", located in Jerusalem, served what purpose from 1948 to 1967?

345

ANSWERS

CURRENT
EVENTS 1205. ► The "Mafdal" or National Religious Party.

ARTS &
CULTURES 1206. ► Flo Ziegfield and his "Ziegfield Follies".

PEOPLE 1207. ► Moses Maimonides (Rambam).

HISTORY 1208. ► Because the Israelites themselves were strangers in Egypt.

HISTORY 1209. ► From Hiram, King of Tyre.

LANGUAGE 1210. ► "Second Law" (since this book repeats much of the preceding books).

GEOGRAPHY 1211. ► It was the border checkpoint between Jordanian and Israeli sections of Jerusalem.

CURRENT
EVENTS

1212. ► Why did President Johnson ask Arthur Goldberg to step down from the Supreme Court?

ARTS &
CULTURES

1213. ► This long-time-famous Jewish actress recently starred in a successfuly Broadway play, based upon a 1942 movie featuring Spencer Tracy and Katherine Hepburn...?

PEOPLE

1214. ► Judah Benjamin was the: Attorney General, Secretary of War and then Secretary of State for what short-lived government?

RELIGION

1215. ► The sounding of the *Shofar* dates back to ancient times. Cite 3 examples of its use in ancient times...?

HISTORY

1216. ► What was the original family name of the Maccabees?

LANGUAGE

1217. ► The meaning of the Hebrew word *Hallelujah* is...?

GEOGRAPHY

1218. ► What is the ancient town of Jewish mystics that has, in recent years, become a center for Israeli artists?

ANSWERS

1212. ► To become the U.S. Representative to the United Nations.

1213. ► Lauren Bacall (in *Woman of the Year*).

1214. ► The Confederate States of America, during the Civil War.

1215. ► Any 3 of these: To warn of enemies; to announce the appointment of a new King; to announce the beginning of a Jubilee year in which slaves were released; during the month before Rosh Hashanah; on Rosh Hashanah; and at the conclusion of "Yom Kippur."

1216. ► Hasmonean.

1217. ► "Praise ye the Lord".

1218. ► Safed.

CURRENT
EVENTS
1219. ► This Jewish public servant won the 1975 Nobel Peace Prize...?

ARTS &
CULTURES
1220. ► An old Jewish expression states "May you live to be 120". What is the origin of this blessing?

PEOPLE
1221. ► Albert Einstein won a Nobel Prize in Physics — it was not for his Theory of Relativity. What was it for?

RELIGION
1222. ► As part of the Rosh Hashanah observance, how do Jews observe the ancient ritual where they symbolically get rid of their sins?

HISTORY
1223. ► Moses was raised as a follower of this religion...?

LANGUAGE
1224. ► What is the literal translation of "Torah"?

GEOGRAPHY
1225. ► This river divided Palestine...?

ANSWERS

CURRENT
EVENTS

1219. ► **Henry Kissinger.**

ARTS &
CULTURES

1220. ► **The Bible says that Moses lived to be 120.**

PEOPLE

1221. ► **The Photo-Electric Effect.**

RELIGION

1222. ► **They throw their sins into a body of water — river, stream, sea, etc.**

HISTORY

1223. ► **Egyptian idol worshipping.**

LANGUAGE

1224. ► **"Instruction".**

GEOGRAPHY

1225. ► **The Jordan River.**

CURRENT
EVENTS

1226. ▶ The position of Chief Rabbi of Israel is held by how many people at the same time?

ARTS &
CULTURES

1227. ▶ He was the Jewish Grand Prix driver from South Africa who won the world championship in 1979...?

PEOPLE

1228. ▶ Casimir Funk was a noted Polish Jewish biochemist who discovered this group of familiar substances, used by health conscious individuals in their everyday life...?

RELIGION

1229. ▶ Who were the people that this Biblical figure killed when he brought the house down?

HISTORY

1230. ▶ Solomon's most famous non-Jewish wife was the daughter of a harsh ruler from this country...?

LANGUAGE

1231. ▶ Why do friends often inscribe Mizpah on rings and ornaments that they give away to friends when they part?

GEOGRAPHY

1232. ▶ A city in Pennsylvania is named after this ancient city...?

ANSWERS

CURRENT
EVENTS 1226. ▶ Two — a Chief Rabbi for the Ashkenazi Jews and a Chief Rabbi for the Sephardic Jews.

ARTS &
CULTURES 1227. ▶ Jody Scheckter.

PEOPLE 1228. ▶ Vitamins.

RELIGION 1229. ▶ The Philistines.

HISTORY 1230. ▶ Egypt. (She was Pharaoh's daughter.)

LANGUAGE 1231. ▶ This was the name given to the column of stone next to Jacob and Laban when they parted.

GEOGRAPHY 1232. ▶ Bethlehem.

CURRENT EVENTS   **1233.** ► The approximate Jewish population of France is...?

ARTS & CULTURES   **1234.** ► Roberta Peters is a specialized Jewish singer in this area...?

PEOPLE   **1235.** ► This Jewish scientist was the first American to win a Nobel Prize. It was awarded for his measurement of the speed of light...?

RELIGION   **1236.** ► The Biblical importance of the "Land of Goshen" is...?

HISTORY   **1237.** ► Who is credited with creating the Hebrew calendar as we know it today?

LANGUAGE   **1238.** ► When a *dreidel* lands on the side that reads *shin* it means the player is entitled to...?

GEOGRAPHY   **1239.** ► This archeological museum located in Jerusalem is named after a famous New York family whose patriarch was an oil tycoon...?

ANSWERS

1253. ► 650,000.

1234. ► An opera soprano.

1235. ► Albert Michelson.

1236. ► It was the part of Egypt where the
Israelites lived (Genesis).

1237. ► Hillel II.

1238. ► "Put in" or *Schtell*).

1239. ► The Rockefeller Museum.

CURRENT
EVENTS   **1240.** ► What event took place in Europe on September 6, 1972, that shocked the civilized world?

ARTS &
CULTURES   **1241.** ► This famous Jewish writer created the original story that the movie *Yentl* was based upon...?

PEOPLE   **1242.** ► This recent U.S. Treasury Secretary converted from Judaism to Presbyterianism when he was younger...?

RELIGION   **1243.** ► The Bible refers to seven types of agricultural foodstuffs that Israel is blessed with. Name four...?

HISTORY   **1244.** ► Which two Biblical animals spoke?

LANGUAGE   **1245.** ► *Purim* in English means?

GEOGRAPHY   **1246.** ► This special zoo in Jerusalem houses most of the animals mentioned in the Bible and is called...?

ANSWERS

1240. ▶ Eleven Israeli athletes were murdered at the Olympic Games in Munich.

1241. ▶ Isaac Bashevis Singer (he wrote *Yentl the Yeshiva Boy*).

1242. ▶ Michael Blumenthal.

1243. ▶ Any four of these: Barley, wheat, figs, honey, olives, pomegranates, milk.

1244. ▶ The snake (spoke to Eve) and the ass (spoke to Balaam).

1245. ▶ "Lots" (representing Haman's drawing of lots to decide the day upon which to destroy the Jews).

1246. ▶ The Biblical Zoo.

CURRENT
EVENTS
1247. ► A long time Comptroller of the City of New York, he later became that city's first Jewish Mayor...?

ARTS &
CULTURES
1248. ► What do the Jewish actors, Gene Barry, Paul Michael Glazer, Jessica Walters, Barry Newman, Jack Lord and Peter Falk have in common?

PEOPLE
1249. ► The Jewish founder of this famous New York department store donated over $20 million worth of art to the Metropolitan Museum of Art...?

RELIGION
1250. ► Why do many Jews symbolically schedule Confirmation ceremonies on *Shavuoth*?

HISTORY
1251. ► The "Jewish Brigade of Palestinian and Stateless Jews", was formed in WWII and fought in this region?

LANGUAGE
1252. ► The Yiddish term *Shandeh* means...?

GEOGRAPHY
1253. ► This major Israeli city is surrounded by valleys...?

ANSWERS

1247. ► **Abraham Beame.**

1248. ► **They have all played detectives on T.V.**

1249. ► **Benjamin Altman.**

1250. ► **Because this is the day that the Jewish people received the Torah from G-d.**

1251. ► **Europe. (They also aided in the rescue of Holocaust survivors.)**

1252. ► **A shame.**

1253. ► **Jerusalem.**

CURRENT
EVENTS
    1254. ► The Jewish population of the U.S.A. makes up approximately what percentage of world Jewry?

ARTS &
·CULTURES
    1255. ► Tevye, the main character in *Fiddler on the Roof*, was employed as a...?

PEOPLE
    1256. ► This noted Jewish scientist revolutionized the early conception of the physical universe...?

RELIGION
    1257. ► What are the traditional four questions asked at the Seder?

HISTORY
    1258. ► He was the first President of Israel...?

LANGUAGE
    1259. ► The Yiddish expression *farblondjet* refers to this state of mind...?

GEOGRAPHY
    1260. ► This American state has the smallest Jewish population...?

ANSWERS

1254. ► Forty percent.

1255. ► Milkman.

1256. ► Albert Einstein.

1257. ► Why do we eat unleavened bread on this night?; Why do we eat bitter herbs on Passover?; Why do we dip the *carpas* in the salt water and the *maaror* in the *haroset*?; and Why do we sit in reclining position at the Seder?

1258. ► Chaim Weizman.

1259. ► Mixed up.

1260. ► Wyoming (home to approximately 360 Jews).

CURRENT
EVENTS

1261. ► Which of the two major categories of Jews outnumbers the other by about 14 to 1?

ARTS &
CULTURES

1262. ► This famous Jewish ventriloquist works with a puppet named Lambchop...?

PEOPLE

1263. ► On April 9, 1948, who were the two parties to this following conversation concerning Palestine: "The choice for our people, Mr. President, is between Statehood and extermination"...?

RELIGION

1264. ► Why has it been asserted that the Ten Commandments are really only nine?

HISTORY

1265. ► What was the only reason for Israel's withdrawal of forces from Sinai, in March of 1957?

LANGUAGE

1266. ► "Amen" literally translates into...?

GEOGRAPHY

1267. ► Goldenberg's is the best-known Jewish eatery in this foreign city, but it recently gained infamy when struck with a terrorist attack...?

ANSWERS

1261. ► The Ashkenazim.

1262. ► Shari Lewis.

1263. ► Dr. Chaim Weizmann speaking to President Harry S Truman.

1264. ► Because the First Commandment is really a statement of fact and not a command: "I am the Lord thy G-d, who brought thee out of the land of Egypt, out of the house of bondage".

1265. ► Due to U.S. pressure.

1266. ► So be it.

1267. ► Paris, France.

CURRENT
EVENTS   1268. ► Why were U.S. troops put on world-
wide alert on October 26, 1973?

ARTS &
CULTURES   1269. ► The Jewish writer, Boris Pasternak,
created this famous doctor in his book
of the same name...?

PEOPLE   1270. ► This Jewish industrialist was known as
the "Henry Ford of France"...?

RELIGION   1271. ► Why are women excluded from the
main part of an Orthodox Synagogue's
sitting area during services?

HISTORY   1272. ► This modern nation may be more than
half Jewish in its hereditary bloodlines,
but not in its religion. What is the
reason for this phenomenon?

LANGUAGE   1273. ► The Yiddish word *bubkes* means...?

GEOGRAPHY   1274. ► Where is "Biro-bidjan" located and
what was it set aside for?

ANSWERS

CURRENT
EVENTS **1268.** ▶ **Over concern that the Soviet Union was planning to introduce its military forces into the "Yom Kippur War", aiding Egypt in their losing battle against Israel.**

ARTS &
CULTURES **1269.** ▶ **Doctor Zhivago.**

PEOPLE **1270.** ▶ **Auto manufacturer André Gustave Citröen.**

RELIGION **1271.** ▶ **Because they might possibly distract the men's attention from the Prayer Service.**

HISTORY **1272.** ▶ **Spain, because of the forced conversions during the Inquisition.**

LANGUAGE **1273.** ▶ **"Nothing".**

GEOGRAPHY **1274.** ▶ **Located in the eastern U.S.S.R., this area was intended as a Jewish Republic after the Bolshevik Revolution. (The area still exists, but the idea was never forcefully implemented.)**

CURRENT
EVENTS

1275. ► Which two Arab countries launched simultaneous attacks on Israel, beginning the 1973 Yom Kippur War?

ARTS &
CULTURES

1276. ► Tevye, of *Fiddler on the Roof*, had how many daughters?

PEOPLE

1277. ► This Tennessee born Jew made the *New York Times* the most powerful newspaper in America...?

RELIGION

1278. ► How many days did the creation of the world take, according to Genesis?

HISTORY

1279. ► The date November 29, 1947, is significant in Palestine's history because...?

LANGUAGE

1280. ► In Yiddish, what does *Yichus* refer to?

GEOGRAPHY

1281. ► The "Mountain of God" or "Horeb" are other names for this famous mountain...?

ANSWERS

1275. ▶ Syria and Egypt.

1276. ▶ Five.

1277. ▶ Adolph S. Ochs.

1278. ▶ Six.

1279. ▶ It was the day of the "U.N. Resolution on the Partition of Palestine", granting recognition to the Jewish state.

1280. ▶ Good family background.

1281. ▶ Mount Sinai.

CURRENT
EVENTS
1282. ► This agency has been responsible for the planting of well over 100 million trees in Israel and they are still active in this endeavor...?

ARTS &
CULTURES
1283. ► This Jewish character in a famous play said: "Sufference is the badge of all our Tribe"...?

PEOPLE
1284. ► This Jewish winner of the 1908 Nobel Prize in medicine and physiology, for his discovery of a cure for syphilis, was the most eminent microbiologist at the turn of the century...?

RELIGION
1285. ► According to Jewish Law, in what country are Jews forbidden to settle?

HISTORY
1286. ► How much time after Israel's announcement of Independence did the Arab states wait before starting their "War of Liberation"?

LANGUAGE
1287. ► What does "Messiah" translate into...?

GEOGRAPHY
1288. ► This European country was the first to abolish the Pope's order that all Jews wear "Badges of Shame"...?

ANSWERS

CURRENT EVENTS   **1282.** ► **The Jewish National Fund.**

ARTS & CULTURES   **1283.** ► **Shylock.**

PEOPLE   **1284.** ► **Paul Ehrlich.**

RELIGION   **1285.** ► **Egypt (because of its enslavement of the ancient Jewish people).**

HISTORY   **1286.** ► **One day.**

LANGUAGE   **1287.** ► **"The anointed one".**

GEOGRAPHY   **1288.** ► **Austria.**

CURRENT
EVENTS

1289. ► What two American Presidents wrote an article together that appeared in the February 1983 *Readers' Digest*, and stated that Israel's West Bank settlement policy is the main obstacle to peace among the moderate Arab countries?

ARTS &
CULTURES

1290. ► This Jewish mellow singer-songwriter wrote "You've Got a Friend" and "It's Too Late"...?

PEOPLE

1291. ► He founded the "Irgun", organized "illegal immigration" to Palestine, and believed that large-scale Jewish immigration and settlement in a Jewish state, were inevitable...?

RELIGION

1292. ► This Biblical quotation: "Not by bread alone doth man live", is found in which of the Five Books of Moses?

HISTORY

1293. ► How many years did King David reign?

LANGUAGE

1294. ► The *Ner Tamid*, present in all Synagogues, refers to this...?

GEOGRAPHY

1295. ► Jerusalem is sometimes called "The Golden" because...?

ANSWERS

1289. ▶ Presidents Gerald Ford and Jimmy Carter.

1290. ▶ Carole King.

1291. ▶ Zev Jabotinsky.

1292. ▶ Deuteronomy.

1293. ▶ Forty years.

1294. ▶ The "Eternal Light" (it is always lit and is usually positioned above the raised platform in front of the Congregation).

1295. ▶ The houses there are built with stones that have a golden color that glow and reflect the rays of the sun and moon.

CURRENT
EVENTS

1296. ► This Jewish politician's wife resigned from her job as a business consultant, to prevent the appearance of a conflict between her activities and her husband's...?

ARTS &
CULTURES

1297. ► Which Jewish comic actor was originally named Walter Matuskainschayak?

PEOPLE

1298. ► This famous Jewish lawyer said: "To be good Americans we must be better Jews, and to be better Jews we must become Zionists"...?

RELIGION

1299. ► The Hebrew calendar year indicates the number of years that have passed since...?

HISTORY

1300. ► Baruch Spinoza, the noted 17th century pihlosopher, is most remembered in Jewish circles because he was the only Jew to have had this happen to him...?

LANGUAGE

1301. ► What does the word *Kosher* translate to?

GEOGRAPHY

1302. ► The Parliament of Israel is convened in this building...?

ANSWERS

1296. ► **Jacob Javits.**

1297. ► **Walter Matthau.**

1298. ► **Louis D. Brandeis.**

1299. ► **The Biblical creation of the world.**

1300. ► **He was excommunicated.**

1301. ► **"Fit".**

1302. ► **The Knesset building.**

CURRENT
EVENTS
1303. ► What was Archbishop Capucci, of the Greek Catholic Church in Jerusalem, arrested for?

ARTS &
CULTURES
1304. ► What is the number of days in the typical Israeli work week?

PEOPLE
1305. ► This American social worker founded the Jewish women's movement Hadassah...?

RELIGION
1306. ► What is the significance of the "Eternal Light", always burning in a Synagogue?

HISTORY
1307. ► 133 C.E. is significant in Jewish history because...?

LANGUAGE
1308. ► The name "Moses", according to Bible etymology, means...?

GEOGRAPHY
1309. ► When the Roman Emperor Hadrian conquered this Jewish city in 135 C.E., he renamed it "Aelia Capitolina". What was the original Jewish name?

ANSWERS

CURRENT EVENTS 1303. ► Smuggling arms to Arab terrorists in Israel.

ARTS & CULTURES 1304. ► Six days (Sunday through Friday).

PEOPLE 1305. ► Henrietta Szold.

RELIGION 1306. ► It symbolizes the Jewish people's lasting faith in the Bible and the Jewish religion.

HISTORY 1307. ► It was the start of Bar Kochba's revolt, and the last period of Jewish independence and statehood until present times.

LANGUAGE 1308. ► "Drawn from the water".

GEOGRAPHY 1309. ► Jerusalem.

CURRENT
EVENTS   1310. ► What country, after bloody fighting, expelled the P.L.O. in 1970?

ARTS &
CULTURES   1311. ► This Jewish baseball player refused to pitch the first game of the 1965 World Series because it fell on Yom Kippur?

PEOPLE   1312. ► He was the originator of Political Zionism....?

RELIGION   1313. ► The Hebrew calendar is based on what cycle?

HISTORY   1314. ► What was so remarkable concerning the circumstances surrounding the birth of the Biblical figure Isaac?

LANGUAGE   1315. ► What does the Yiddish word *landsman* refer to?

GEOGRAPHY   1316. ► The "Dead Sea Scrolls" are stored in this Shrine...?

ANSWERS

CURRENT
EVENTS   1310. ► Jordan.

ARTS &
CULTURES   1311. ► Sandy Koufax.

PEOPLE   1312. ► Theodore Herzl.

RELIGION   1313. ► The Lunar Cycle.

HISTORY   1314. ► The age of his parents (Abraham was
                              100 years old and Sarah was 90 years
                              old).

LANGUAGE   1315. ► One who comes from the same village
                              as you do.

GEOGRAPHY   1316. ► The "Shrine of the Book".

376

CURRENT
EVENTS   1317. ► What is the name of the Israeli manu-
factured supersonic jet fighter?

ARTS &
CULTURES   1318. ► When Elizabeth Taylor converted to
Judaism, which husband was it for?

PEOPLE   1319. ► This Polish born Jew was famous for
her fine and extensive line of
cosmetics...?

RELIGION   1320. ► What is the main purpose of the
"koshering" process for meats?

HISTORY   1321. ► On the same day that Jerusalem was
captured and rescued by the British
what similar significant occurence
happened in ancient Jewish history?

LANGUAGE   1322. ► Yiddish is a combination of what two
languages?

GEOGRAPHY   1323. ► This famous Roman monument was
constructed in Rome to celebrate the
destruction of Jerusalem...?

ANSWERS

CURRENT
EVENTS   1317. ► The "Kfir".

ARTS &
CULTURES   1318. ► Eddie Fischer.

PEOPLE   1319. ► Helena Rubenstein.

RELIGION   1320. ► To rid the meat of its blood.

HISTORY   1321. ► Jerusalem was rescued from the
                   Syrians by the Maccabees.

LANGUAGE   1322. ► Hebrew and German.

GEOGRAPHY 1323. ► The Arch of Titus.

CURRENT
EVENTS

1324. ► What was the name of the Israeli town where 21 school children were killed and 70 wounded, on May 15th, 1975?

ARTS &
CULTURES

1325. ► This famous old-time Jewish boxing coach, managed Max Schmeling and was famous for the quote: "We wuz robbed"...?

PEOPLE

1326. ► The *New York Times* is presently controlled by this distinguished Jewish clan...?

RELIGION

1327. ► A glass is crushed by the groom after a Jewish wedding for this reason...?

HISTORY

1328. ► The Territorialist Movement was founded in 1902, during the early years of the Zionist movement. What was its purpose?

LANGUAGE

1329. ► What was the "Numerus Clausus", used in most European countries before World War II?

GEOGRAPHY

1330. ► Many towns in Israel have a street named after the most famous Israeli poet, also known as the "National Poet"...?

ANSWERS

1324. ▶ Ma'alot.

1325. ▶ Joe Jacobs (known as "Yussel the Muscle").

1326. ▶ The Sulzbergers.

1327. ▶ To remember the destruction of the Holy Temple in Jerusalem.

1328. ▶ To find a homeland for a Jewish state. (This group was looking for alternatives to the unsuccessful Uganda Project, sponsored by the British).

1329. ▶ The law that limited the number of Jewish students allowed to enroll in universities.

1330. ▶ Bialik Street.

CURRENT
EVENTS
    1331. ► In commemoration of the U.S. Bicentennial, the City of Philadelphia, gave Jerusalem a replica of this most cherished symbol...?

ARTS &
CULTURES
    1332. ► This Jewish sports figure is well known as "The Mouth" and has an abrasive style...?

PEOPLE   1333. ► The Jewish Blaustein family founded a U.S. oil firm called The American Oil Co. It is better known as...?

RELIGION   1334. ► The *Tashlich* ceremony is practiced by Orthodox Jews and occurs on the first day of Rosh Hashanah. What is it?

HISTORY   1335. ► In 1939, Albert Einstein sent a letter to Franklin D. Roosevelt that ultimately changed the course of history. What proposal was made in the letter?

LANGUAGE   1336. ► The meaning of *Yom* is...?

GEOGRAPHY   1337. ► Which Arab country is closest to Jerusalem?

ANSWERS

1331. ► The Liberty Bell.

1332. ► Howard Cosell.

PEOPLE 1333. ► Amoco.

RELIGION 1334. ► Jews go to bodies of water and recite Prayers of Penitence, thereby "casting off" all sins into the water. (This occurs between the morning and afternoon services.)

HISTORY 1335. ► The program to develop the atomic bomb, before the Nazis did.

LANGUAGE 1336. ► "Day".

GEOGRAPHY 1337. ► Jordan.

CURRENT
EVENTS

1338. ► What two major issues — one in politics and one in religion — are Israelis divided on?

ARTS &
CULTURES

1339. ► Which member of the Beatles has a Jewish wife?

PEOPLE

1340. ► This Nazi war criminal made a daring escape from a Rome hospital in 1977?

RELIGION

1341. ► Exactly when does the "Sabbath" begin?

HISTORY

1342. ► What were *Megiddo* and *Hazor*?

LANGUAGE

1343. ► What does the Yiddish expression *Gut Yomtov* mean?

GEOGRAPHY

1344. ► Israel's most renowned institute of technology, located on Mount Carmel, is called...?

ANSWERS

CURRENT EVENTS

1338. ▶ In politics: What to do with the territories occupied since 1967. In religion: Whether or not to separate religion from government.

ARTS & CULTURES

1339. ▶ Paul McCartney (married to Linda Eastman).

PEOPLE

1340. ▶ Nazi war criminal Kappler.

RELIGION

1341. ▶ At sundown on Friday evening.

HISTORY

1342. ▶ Fortresses built by King Solomon.

LANGUAGE

1343. ▶ Happy Holiday.

GEOGRAPHY

1344. ▶ Technion.

384

CURRENT
EVENTS   1345. ► *Yom Yerushalayim* is a recently created holiday in Israel. What does it celebrate?

ARTS &
CULTURES   1346. ► This Jewish actor starred in the movies *Cast a Giant Shadow* and *Victory at Entebbe*...?

PEOPLE   1347. ► Jewish financier Jacob Schiff was affiliated with this investment banking firm...?

RELIGION   1348. ► The three Patriarchs are...?

HISTORY   1349. ► What was the name of the famous ship carrying immigrants to Israel, that was captured by the British in 1947, and sent back to Germany?

LANGUAGE   1350. ► What type of immigration movement was *Aliyah Bet*, which operated during the British mandate in Palestine?

GEOGRAPHY   1351. ► Name any three Gates to the Old City of Jerusalem...?

ANSWERS

CURRENT
EVENTS 1345. ► "Jerusalem Day" celebrates the day Jerusalem was liberated and reunited during the Six-Day War.

ARTS &
CULTURES 1346. ► Kirk Douglas.

PEOPLE 1347. ► Kuhn Loeb.

RELIGION 1348. ► Abraham, Isaac and Jacob.

HISTORY 1349. ► The *Exodus, 1947*.

LANGUAGE 1350. ► It was an "illegal" immigration movement bringing Jews to Palestine despite the British prohibition.

GEOGRAPHY 1351. ► Any of these three: Damascus, Jaffa, Zion, Lions, Dung, Herod and the Gate of Mercy (which is closed until the "Messiah" arrives).

CURRENT
EVENTS   1352. ► The ownership of most of the land in Israel is by...?

ARTS &
CULTURES   1353. ► This Jewish writer is the most popular science fiction writer in America today...?

PEOPLE   1354. ► This South American Jewish editor was jailed without trial for one year, because of his newspaper's controversial views...?

RELIGION   1355. ► This Prophet is the guest at all Passover Seders...?

HISTORY   1356. ► The symbol of the Tribe of Judah is...?

LANGUAGE   1357. ► *Hedunya* (in Hebrew) and *Naden* (in Yiddish) are words for a practice which has gone out of favor in the modern world. What is this?

GEOGRAPHY   1358. ► In 1903, this location in East Africa was suggested by the British government as a Jewish settlement area...?

ANSWERS

CURRENT
EVENTS

1352. ► The government. (Only 10% is in the hands of the private sector.)

ARTS &
CULTURES

1353. ► Isaac Asimov.

PEOPLE

1354. ► Jacobo Timerman.

RELIGION

1355. ► Elijah.

HISTORY

1356. ► The Lion.

LANGUAGE

1357. ► A dowry.

GEOGRAPHY

1358. ► Uganda.

CURRENT
EVENTS   1359. ► Golda Meir's Defense Minister in 1974 was...?

ARTS &
CULTURES   1360. ► When Marilyn Monroe converted to Judaism, which husband was it for?

PEOPLE   1361. ► He said: "They shall beat their swords into plowshares and their spears into pruning hooks. Nation shall not lift sword against nation neither shall they learn war any more"...?

RELIGION   1362. ► This holiday comes five days after *Yom Kippur*...?

HISTORY   1363. ► What was the attitude of the Soviet Union regarding the establishment of Israel, after World War II?

LANGUAGE   1364. ► The Yiddish word *Maven* refers to...?

GEOGRAPHY   1365. ► This mountain facing Jerusalem has an ancient cemetery on its grounds...?

ANSWERS

CURRENT
EVENTS   **1359.** ▶ **Moshe Dayan.**

ARTS &
CULTURES   **1360.** ▶ **Arthur Miller.**

PEOPLE   **1361.** ▶ **Isaiah.**

RELIGION   **1362.** ▶ **Succoth.**

HISTORY   **1363.** ▶ **Strongly in favor.**

LANGUAGE   **1364.** ▶ **An expert (from the Hebrew "he who understands").**

GEOGRAPHY   **1365.** ▶ **The Mount of Olives.**

CURRENT
EVENTS   1366. ► The most important natural resource of Israel is...?

ARTS &
CULTURES   1367. ► This hilarious Jewish comedian-musician was born with the name Allen Stuart Koenigsberg...?

PEOPLE   1368. ► This distinguished Jewish public servant wrote the widely respected book *Nuclear Weapons and Foreign Policy*, which disputed the concept of "massive retaliation" and advocated the "flexible response" strategy"...?

RELIGION   1369. ► The first person born on earth was...?

HISTORY   1370. ► Why was this Biblical figure thrown into the lion's den, and what happened to him there?

LANGUAGE   1371. ► What is the ancient Hebrew term used for a marriage contract, that stipulates the husband's obligations to his wife?

GEOGRAPHY   1372. ► Where did Moses receive the Ten Commandments?

ANSWERS

<table>
<tr><td>CURRENT EVENTS</td><td>1366.</td><td>▶ The mineral wealth of the Dead Sea.</td></tr>
<tr><td>ARTS & CULTURES</td><td>1367.</td><td>▶ Woody Allen.</td></tr>
<tr><td>PEOPLE</td><td>1368.</td><td>▶ Henry Kissinger.</td></tr>
<tr><td>RELIGION</td><td>1369.</td><td>▶ Cain.</td></tr>
<tr><td>HISTORY</td><td>1370.</td><td>▶ Daniel was being punished by the King of Babylon, and the God of Israel intervened and saved him in the den.</td></tr>
<tr><td>LANGUAGE</td><td>1371.</td><td>▶ Ketubbah.</td></tr>
<tr><td>GEOGRAPHY</td><td>1372.</td><td>▶ Mt. Sinai.</td></tr>
</table>

CURRENT
EVENTS

1373. ► Which government was surprised and outraged when it became known that anti-Semitic groups within its borders were circulating a dice and board game featuring the objective of getting the pieces, representing Jews, into squares named after Nazi concentration camps?

ARTS &
CULTURES

1374. ► This New York City hospital is named after an Englsih born Jew...?

PEOPLE

1375. ► The U.S. President who recognized Israel was...?

RELIGION

1376. ► How did Samson die?

HISTORY

1377. ► What major wave of anti-semitism began in 1881, and where did it occur...?

LANGUAGE

1378. ► What does *Trefah* refer to in food?

GEOGRAPHY

1379. ► Jerusalem's war monument includes a *Davidka*, which is...?

ANSWERS

CURRENT EVENTS 1373. ► The West German government (they confiscated these games of the Neo-Nazi and right wing groups).

ARTS & CULTURES 1374. ► Montefiore Hospital.

PEOPLE 1375. ► Harry S. Truman.

RELIGION 1376. ► He died with the Philistines when he toppled their temple upon them and himself.

HISTORY 1377. ► The Russian Czar's *pogroms* against the Jews, throughout Russia.

LANGUAGE 1378. ► "Non-kosher" and, therefore, forbidden for consumption.

GEOGRAPHY 1379. ► An Israeli modified mortar gun. (This weapon was important to Israel's success in the 1948 War of Independence.)

CURRENT
EVENTS

1380. ► The *Irgun* weapons boat *Altalena* was named after this person...?

ARTS &
CULTURES

1381. ► This special bread is eaten on the "Sabbath"...?

PEOPLE

1382. ► This Jewish politician won the U.S. Senate seat vacated by Herbert Lehman, and served four terms in office...?

RELIGION

1383. ► According to the Bible, whom did G-d say this to: "Raise your eyes and look...to the north and south, to the east and west, for I give all the land that you see to you and your offspring forever"...?

HISTORY

1384. ► What was the highest authority in Palestine called, during the British Mandate?

LANGUAGE

1385. ► What is a *Gniza*?

GEOGRAPHY

1386. ► The village of Deganyah, founded in 1909, was the first example of this...?

ANSWERS

CURRENT
EVENTS 1380. ► Zev Jabotinsky (it was his pen name while writing for the Russian press).

ARTS &
CULTURES 1381. ► *Challah*.

PEOPLE 1382. ► Jacob Javits.

RELIGION 1383. ► Abraham.

HISTORY 1384. ► The British High Commissioner.

LANGUAGE 1385. ► A depository in a Synagogue for unusable texts.

GEOGRAPHY 1386. ► A kibbutz.

CURRENT
EVENTS

1387. ► This Pope was the first to renounce the actions of the Catholic Church during the Spanish Inquisition, stating that they were wrong to kill the thousands of Jews that refused to convert to Catholicism...?

ARTS &
CULTURES

1388. ► This award-winning Jewish actor starred in a 1976 mystery movie involving a fugitive Nazi war criminal...?

PEOPLE

1389. ► This great anthropologist was a professor at Columbia and a curator at the American Museum of Natural History and was famous for his works which showed that there were no fundamental differences in thinking or intelligence between the races. He was also known for his vehement stand against Nazi racial theories...?

RELIGION

1390. ► Donations are collected at Jewish funerals because of this Biblical reference...?

HISTORY

1391. ► What is the "Joint"?

LANGUAGE

1392. ► Who are the "Miluim"?

GEOGRAPHY

1393. ► The Cave of Elijah is located in this mountain...?

ANSWERS

1387. ► Pope John Paul II, in November of 1983.

1388. ► Dustin Hoffman (in *Marathon Man*).

1389. ► Franz Boas.

1390. ► The Biblical injunction that "charity delivers from death".

1391. ► American Jewish Joint Distribution — an organization to assist Jews worldwide.

1392. ► The Israeli Army reserves.

1393. ► Mount Carmel.

CURRENT
EVENTS   1394. ► What type of jury system does Israel have?

ARTS &
CULTURES   1395. ► Laura Z. Hobsen is famous in American Jewish Literature for her novel on social anti-Semitism. What was its title?

PEOPLE   1396. ► What famous Jewish-Czech novelist wrote *Amerika, The Trial,* and *The Castle?*

RELIGION   1397. ► Chanukah occurs in this Hebrew month...?

HISTORY   1398. ► What ancient group controlled Jerusalem prior to its becoming the ancient capital of Israel?

LANGUAGE   1399. ► *Zoftig* refers to...?

GEOGRAPHY   1400. ► The "Green Line" refers to a cease-fire line between these two nations...?

PEOPLE   1401. ► This American Jewish public servant enjoys bantering with his constituents and has popularized the question: "So how am I doin'?"...?

ANSWERS

CURRENT
EVENTS   **1394.** ► **There are no juries — rather panels of one, three or five judges.**

ARTS &
CULTURES   **1395.** ► *Gentlemen's Agreement.*

PEOPLE   **1396.** ► **Franz Kafka.**

RELIGION   **1397.** ► **Kislev.**

HISTORY   **1398.** ► **The Jebusites (before 1000 B.C.E.)**

LANGUAGE   **1399.** ► **A "full-bodied, well put together" woman.**

GEOGRAPHY   **1400.** ► **Israel and Jordan.**

PEOPLE   **1401.** ► **Mayor Ed Koch (of New York City).**

THE END

of *Trivia Judaica* – *Book I*

Look for Book II, Coming Soon!!

The Jewish Trivia and Information Book™ II
Trivia Judaica™ II

Orders will be accepted in advance of the first printing of Trivia Judaica™ II

by using the forms in the last pages of this book.

ALSO COMING SOON: The *Jewish Trivia and Information Game*™

Orders for the *Jewish Trivia and Information Game*™ will be accepted in advance of our limited public distribution, by using the forms on the last pages of this book.

STEIMATZKY
New York   Jerusalem   Tel Aviv

Steimatzky Books of Special Interest